The Marketing Yellow Pages

The Marketing Yellow Pages

A Guide to Online Marketing Resources

First Edition

Chris M. Vogl

iUniverse, Inc.
New York Lincoln Shanghai

The Marketing Yellow Pages
A Guide to Online Marketing Resources

iUniverse, Inc.

For information address:
iUniverse, Inc.
2021 Pine Lake Road, Suite 100
Lincoln, NE 68512
www.iuniverse.com

ISBN: 0-595-28132-X

Printed in the United States of America

Contents

Introduction xv

Section 1 Locating Websites 1

- *1.1 Locating Websites. 1*
- *1.2 About Web Addresses 2*
- *1.3 Parts of World Wide Web Addresses 2*
- *1.4 Eliminating Extended Portions of Web Addresses 3*
- *1.5 Know Your Browser 3*
- *1.6 Learn How to Use the Features of Your Browser. 4*
- *1.7 Using Search Engines 4*
- *1.8 Name & Subject Searches 5*
- *1.9 Using Your Browser (web resources) 5*

Section 2 Consumer Protection Sites. 7

- *2.1 Consumer Protection Sites. 7*

Section 3 Marketing Information 10

- *3.1 Brand Building (products & services) .10*
- *3.2 Competitive Intelligence 12*
- *3.3 Consulting Services. 13*
- *3.4 Employment Information 14*
- *3.5 Market Analysis Reports 14*
- *3.6 Market Analysis (target) 15*
- *3.7 Marketing Information (General) 15*
- *3.8 Marketing Information (manufacturers) 21*
- *3.9 Marketing Planning & Strategy 21*
- *3.10 Marketing Project Coordination 22*

- *3.11 Market Research & Information* 23
- *3.12 Marketing Research (tools & resources)* 26
- *3.13 Market Segmentation* 27
- *3.14 Marketing Services (purchasing)* 28
- *3.15 Multicultural Marketing* 29
- *3.16 Naming (businesses, products, or services)* 30
- *3.17 Positioning (businesses, products & services)* 31
  Also see Building Brands (this section)
- *3.18 Press Release Writing* 31
  Also see Public Relations/Press Releases (this section)
- *3.19 Pricing Information* 32
- *3.20 Public Relations/Press Releases* 33
- *3.21 Trade Show Information* 36
- *3.22 Web-Related Marketing Statistics* 37
- *3.23 Yellow Page Advertising (ad design services)* 37
- *3.24 Yellow Page Advertising (management services)* 37

Section 4 Business Information (general) 39
- *4.1 Background Checks* 39
- *4.2 Branding (business names)* 40
- *4.3 Business Counseling* 41
- *4.4 Business Information (general)* 42
- *4.5 Business Information (industry specific)* 45
- *4.6 Business Information (new businesses)* 47
- *4.7 Business Intelligence* 47
- *4.8 Business Plans & Related Information* 48
- *4.9 Business Products (locating)* 49
- *4.10 Buyers Guides* 50
- *4.11 Competitive Intelligence (online)* 50
- *4.12 Consulting Services* 51
- *4.13 Copyrights* 51
- *4.14 Display and Merchandising Products* 52
- *4.15 Domain Names & Trademarks* 53

- *4.16 Drop Shipping* *55*
  Also see Order Fulfillment & Warehousing (this section)
- *4.17 Government Contracts* *56*
- *4.18 Order Fulfillment & Warehousing* *56*
- *4.19 Pricing* *58*
- *4.20 Shipping Information & Tracking* *58*
- *4.21 Shipping Services (heavy freight)* *60*
  Also see Shipping Information & Tracking (this section)
  Drop-Shipping (this section)
- *4.22 Supply Chain Management* *61*
- *4.23 Trademarks* *62*
  See Domain Names & Trademarks (this section)

Section 5 Business Information (list resources) 63
- *5.1 Business & Consumer Lists (direct marketing)* *63*
- *5.2 Business & Consumer List Selection (marketing)* *66*
- *5.3 Business Directories* *66*
- *5.4 Database Services (business & consumer)* *67*
- *5.5 Information about Businesses* *67*
- *5.6 List Processing Services* *70*

Section 6 Advertising 72
- *6.1 Ad Design* *72*
- *6.2 Advertising Glossary* *73*
- *6.3 Advertising Information* *73*
- *6.4 Advertising and Marketing Laws* *74*
- *6.5 Advertising Placement Locator* *76*
  Also see Media Search (this section)
- *6.6 Ad Viewing* *77*
- *6.7 Banner Ads (samples)* *78*
- *6.8 E-mail and Ezine Advertising* *78*
- *6.9 Media Search (newspapers, magazines, etc.)* *79*
- *6.10 Web Advertising Information* *81*
- *6.11 Web Advertising Selection* *83*

- *6.12 Web Advertising Services* *83*
- *6.13 Web Advertising Solutions/Products* *85*

Section 7 International Business 86
- *7.1 Advertising Slogan Search* *86*
- *7.2 Conversion Information & Tools* *86*
- *7.3 Demographic Information (international)* *88*
- *7.4 Foreign Countries (information)* *88*
- *7.5 Global Marketing* *90*
- *7.6 Global Publications & Periodicals* *90*
- *7.7 Import/Export (financial services)* *91*
- *7.8 Import/Export (general)* *91*
- *7.9 Import/Export Information* *92*
- *7.10 Import/Export (services & portals)* *97*
- *7.11 Import/Export (tools & services)* *100*
- *7.12 International Business Information* *101*
- *7.13 International Company & Product Information* *103*
- *7.14 International Economics* *103*
- *7.15 International Trademarks* *103*
- *7.16 International Trade Leads (buyers & sellers)* *104*
- *7.17 Market Research Service Locator* *104*
- *7.18 Shipping* *104*
  See Shipping (Business Information Section)
- *7.19 Trade Barriers, Tariffs and Restrictions* *105*
- *7.20 Trade Professionals/Trade Company Recruiting* *105*
- *7.21 Trade Show Information* *106*
- *7.22 Translation Services* *106*
- *7.23 U.K. Marketing, Advertising, and Media* *107*

Section 8 Promotional Materials 109
- *8.1 Communications Materials* *109*
- *8.2 Copywriting Services (sales & marketing)* *110*
- *8.3 Design & Copy Professionals (recruiting)* *112*
- *8.4 Desktop Publishing* *113*

- *8.5 Document Templates* *113*
- *8.6 Graphic Design* *114*
- *8.7 Logo Creation* *114*
- *8.8 Logo Merchandise (promotional products)* *114*
- *8.9 Newsletter Writing Services.* *115*
- *8.10 Photographic Images.* *115*
- *8.11 Photographic Images & Clipart.* *116*
- *8.12 Printing (high volume).* *117*
- *8.13 Printing (promotional materials).* *118*
- *8.14 Printing (signs & lettering).* *118*
- *8.15 Visual Content.* *118*

Section 9 Government Information 120
- *9.1 Business Information and Services* *120*
- *9.2 Census Information* *122*
- *9.3 Demographic Information (international)* *123*
- *9.4 Import/Export* *123*
- *9.5 Selling to the Government.* *127*
- *9.6 Statistical Information* *127*

Section 10 Direct Mail 129
- *10.1 Direct Mail Information* *129*
- *10.2 Direct Mail Planning.* *131*
- *10.3 Direct Mail Quotes* *131*
- *10.4 Direct Mail Service (full-service).* *132*
- *10.5 Mail Order Terminology* *132*
- *10.6 Postal Information* *132*
- *10.7 Post Cards.* *133*

Section 11 Web Marketing Strategy 135
- *11.1 Affiliate Programs* *135*
- *11.2 Bots (using, buying, creating)* *136*
- *11.3 Customer Security* *136*
- *11.4 Demographic Information (web users)* *137*

- *11.5 Direct E-mail* *137*
- *11.6 E-mail List Searches* *139*
- *11.7 E-mail List Tools/Services* *139*
- *11.8 Legal Issues* *140*
- *11.9 Web Marketing Information* *140*
- *11.10 Web Marketing Research* *142*
- *11.11 Web Marketing Terminology* *142*

Section 12 Website Development 144

- *12.1 Content Services* *144*
- *12.2 Customer Incentives* *144*
- *12.3 Databases* *145*
- *12.4 Domain Names (registration)* *145*
- *12.5 Domain Names (selection)* *146*
- *12.6 Payment Processing Information (website)* *147*
- *12.7 Payment Processing (international website sales)* *147*
- *12.8 Payment Processing (website credit card sales)* *148*
- *12.9 Payment & Transaction Processing (digital products)* *150*
- *12.10 Photographic Images* *152*
- *12.11 Web & Internet Terminology* *153*
- *12.12 Website Analysis* *153*
- *12.13 Website Design* *153*
- *12.14 Web Site Development & Planning* *155*
- *12.15 Web Site Personalization* *156*
- *12.16 Website & Online Business Strategy* *157*
- *12.17 Website Surveys* *157*

Section 13 Website Promotion 159

- *13.1 Domain Name Registration Sites* *159*
- *13.2 Website Promotion Information (search engines)* *160*
- *13.3 Website Promotion Services* *162*
- *13.4 Website Promotion Software* *164*

Section 14 Marketing Associations 166

- *14.1 Association Search Sites* *166*
- *14.2 Marketing* *167*
- *14.3 Online Retailers* *169*
- *14.4 Product Development & Management* *169*
- *14.5 Trade Show Search Site* *170*

Section 15 Periodicals 171

- *15.1 Advertising Related* *171*
- *15.2 Catalog Related* *172*
- *15.3 Competitive Intelligence* *173*
- *15.4 Customer Management & Support* *174*
- *15.5 Direct Marketing* *174*
- *15.6 Direct Mail (direct mail design & copy)* *175*
- *15.7 Display & Merchandising Periodicals (retail)* *175*
- *15.8 E-Publications (search tool)* *176*
- *15.9 General Industry Periodicals* *176*
- *15.10 Import/Export Transportation* *177*
- *15.11 Internet & E-business Marketing* *178*
- *15.12 Labels (systems & business forms)* *181*
- *15.13 Marketing-Related Periodicals* *181*
- *15.14 Market Research* *184*
- *15.15 Marketing Software* *184*
- *15.16 Media Search* *185*
- *15.17 Newspaper Searches* *185*
- *15.18 Periodical Information (media searches)* *186*
- *15.19 Product Development & Management* *187*
- *15.20 Sales (sales force)* *188*
- *15.21 Supply Chain Management (software)* *188*
- *15.22 Trade Show Information* *188*
- *15.23 E-mail Newsletters (miscellaneous)* *189*
- *15.24 Miscellaneous Newsletters* *189*
- *15.25 U.K. Marketing Publications* *190*

Section 16 Publications 192

- *16.1 Advertising, Marketing, and Media Directories* *192*
- *16.2 Branding* *194*
- *16.3 Government Information* *194*
- *16.4 Import/Export* *195*
- *16.5 Import/Export Transportation* *195*
- *16.6 International Reference* *196*
- *16.7 Internet Related* *197*
- *16.8 Market Research* *197*
- *16.9 Marketing Terminology* *198*
- *16.10 Product Development* *198*
- *16.11 Publication Search (global)* *199*

Section 17 Software 200

- *17.1 Advertising Planning* *200*
- *17.2 Business Planning* *201*
- *17.3 Catalog Management* *202*
- *17.4 Competitive Intelligence Software* *203*
- *17.5 Customer Service (website software)* *203*
- *17.6 Database Products
  (customer information management)* *204*
- *17.7 Export Software* *204*
- *17.8 Internet & Web Strategy* *205*
- *17.9 Logo Software* *205*
- *17.10 Mailing List Management* *206*
- *17.11 Mail Order & E-commerce* *207*
- *17.12 Marketing Management* *207*
- *17.13 Marketing Planning* *208*
- *17.14 Market Research (online)* *210*
- *17.15 Marketing Strategy* *211*
- *17.16 Merchandising Software* *211*
- *17.17 Pricing* *212*
- *17.18 Product Evaluation* *214*

- *17.19 Project Funding* **214**
- *17.20 Sales Planning* *215*
- *17.21 Sales Strategy* *215*
- *17.22 Sales Tools* *215*
- *17.23 Supply Chain Management* *216*
- *17.24 Survey Software* *216*
- *17.25 Website Promotion* *217*
- *17.26 Website Promotion Management* *219*
- *17.27 Software Selection Sites* *219*

Section 18 Things to Remember **221**
- *18.1 Business and Marketing Advice* *221*
- *18.2 Business and Marketing-Related Services* *223*
- *18.3 Government & Organization Resources* *225*
- *18.4 Import/Export Resources* *227*
- *18.5 Industry-Specific Books & Information* *228*
- *18.6 Industry-Specific Buyers Guides* *230*
- *18.7 Industry-Specific Websites* *230*
- *18.8 Magazine & Periodical Websites* *231*
- *18.9 Trade Associations* *233*
- *18.10 Trade Shows* **234**

Section 19 Glossary Resources **236**
- *19.1 International Economics* *236*
- *19.2 Mail Order Terminology* *236*
- *19.3 Marketing Terminology* *237*
- *19.4 Web & Internet Terminology* *237*
- *19.5 Web Marketing Terminology* *238*

Conclusion **241**

Introduction

The resources that have one or more asterisks (*) in front of the title are select resources. All of the resources in this guide provide useful information, products and/or services. Some, however, are unique, specifically useful, easy to use, or have an attribute that makes them stand out. These resources are marked with one or more asterisk(s).

Some of the resources in this guide are listed more than once. Multiple listings were a practical way to help users find resources that provided information, products and/or services that relate to multiple categories in the table of contents.

Most of the resources in this guide are useful to small businesses. A few of the resources are described as high-end or as being useful to medium-to-large-sized businesses. These resources are higher priced products and/or services. They're useful resources, but some businesses will not find them affordable.

This guide mentions small businesses numerous times. When small businesses are mentioned, the author is thinking of most businesses. Large businesses can afford resources beyond the scope of this guide. Most, however, could benefit from the resources listed.

The table of contents should be sufficient to help you find the information and resources you need. Each new edition of this guide will have improved features for its table of contents.

I sincerely hope that this guide will help you find the resources you need to successfully market products and/or services.

Section 1

Locating
Websites

1.1 LOCATING WEBSITES

If you're an experienced World Wide Web user, the information in this section will be of little interest. The following was added to help occasional or inexperienced web users access the resources listed in this guide.

Detailed information to help you use various web browsers is readily available. You can find books to help you use your browser at bookstores and book retail websites. You can also find related information with your browser's help features and at the websites listed at the end of this section.

Using search engines (search sites) is briefly covered in this section. In some cases, it will be necessary to use more than one search engine to find a website. Bookmarking advanced search pages or saving them as favorites is a practical way to utilize multiple search services. You can perform repeated searches without having to download graphics and features that are commonly associated with the main pages of search sites.

There are numerous books and sources of information related to using the Internet and Web. Consequently, I chose not to go into the subject in detail.

1.2 ABOUT WEB ADDRESSES

All of the resource addresses listed in this guide worked at the time of publication. Unfortunately, Internet and web addresses sometimes change.

The following will help you locate the websites listed in this guide. If you need additional information about web addresses, use your favorite search engine to locate it. I typed *web addresses* in at Yahoo's advanced search page and was presented with numerous resources.

Each website address listed in this guide was given a substantial amount of consideration. Some listings feature extended addresses (http://www.myadddress.com/index), while others contain only basic elements (http://www.myaddress.com).

Extended addresses were used in some listings so you could directly access a useful page in a website. Some of the listed resources are not easy to locate from an index or home page. In such cases, the extended addresses provide an easy method to access specific web pages with useful information and resources. In many cases, they were avoided because the extended portions of website addresses are commonly changed.

The following is an example of an extended address.
Extended web address: (http://www.myaddress.com/index/details).
An extended address takes you to a page inside of a website that provides specific information.

In the following address, the extended portion has been eliminated.
Basic web address: (http://www.myaddress.com).

Basic web addresses usually take you to a main page (home page or index page) of a site that features links or navigation features that enable you to access other pages.

1.3 PARTS OF WORLD WIDE WEB ADDRESSES

(http://www.myaddress.com) is a typical website address

(http) indicates the method for retrieving the page (hyper text transfer protocol)
(www) indicates the type of page (world wide web document)
(myaddress) is the primary domain name you register
(.com) is the top-level domain

1.4 ELIMINATING EXTENDED PORTIONS OF WEB ADDRESSES

If you are having problems locating a listed address, try eliminating the extended portion of the address.

First Attempt: enter http://www.myaddress.com/index

Second Attempt: enter http://www.myaddress.com/

Most of the addresses in this guide will enable you to locate the described resources. Simply type the address into the address bar of your web browser and click on go. In some cases, you might have to use a search engine (search site) to locate a listed website.

1.5 KNOW YOUR BROWSER

Most people that use the web are familiar with their web browser. Internet Explorer and Netscape Navigator are the most commonly used browsers.

If you are unfamiliar with the features of your browser, you might want to consider doing one of the following:

1. Learn how to use the help features of your browser.

2. Buy a users guide for the browser that you are using.

3. Access one of the websites listed at the end of this section. They contain information and tips related to using web browsers.

1.6 Learn How to Use the Features of Your Browser

Knowing how to do the following will help you efficiently utilize the resources listed in this guide.

1. Bookmark web pages or save them as favorites. Bookmarking pages or saving them as favorites will provide you with an easy way to access a website later.

2. Rename pages that you have saved to help you understand what they contain. Sometimes renaming saved pages makes it easier to remember what is offered as various websites.

3. Create folders to help you organize your favorites. Folders are a good way to help you keep track of numerous websites.

4. Find websites that your browser can't locate. In some cases, you can locate websites with a search engine (search site) that you can't find with your browser. Using search sites is a good way to find alternative addresses for the sites listed in this guide. If an address is not working, try using a search site to find an alternative address.

1.7 Using Search Engines

Search engines are useful tools to help you locate the websites that are listed in this guide. Your web browser will locate most of the addresses listed. In some cases, however, you will have to use a search engine to locate a listed website.

If you're serious about using the web, you might want to consider saving an advanced search page as your home page or as a favorite. Doing so enables you to perform searches faster. You won't have to wait for new ads, features, and information to download each time you want to perform a search.

Most of the advanced search pages that are offered by search sites (search engines) have minimal ads and options. They load quicker and some of them enable you to add search criteria to perform searches that are more specific.

I use Yahoo's advanced search feature a lot. It works well but you need to select the *web* option by the search box to make sure it searches the web. Yahoo is a directory service. It's my understanding that standard searches do not search the web unless you select the web option.

One search service (search engine) isn't going to find all the sites you want to access. I also use the advanced search features of Alta Vista and other search sites. Some search engines will locate sites that others won't.

1.8 NAME & SUBJECT SEARCHES

If you have trouble finding a listed site, consider a name and subject search. Many of the advanced search features that are offered by search sites (search engines) enable you to search by multiple criteria.

For instance, if you're having problems accessing http://www.marketingyellowpages.com consider the following:

Enter *marketingyellowpages.com* in the first search field.

Enter *marketing* in the second field.

Click Search.

1.9 USING YOUR BROWSER (WEB RESOURCES)

Beginners Central

Website: http://www.northernwebs.com/bc/

Keywords: Web Browser and Search Tips

Description: Beginners Central offers information related to searching the web, using your web browser and more. The site also features information to help you understand the Internet and web.

Bookmarking Web Pages and Saving Them as Favorites

Scroll down on the listed page and click on the *Bookmarking Your Resources* link in the *Chapter One* link section. The page provides easy-to-follow instructions to help you organize web pages that you visit regularly.

Internet Tutorials

Website: http://library.albany.edu/internet/

Keywords: Web Browser, Search Engine, Internet and Web Tips

Description: Internet Tutorials provide information to help you understand and use the Internet, World Wide Web, search engines and web browsers. The information related to web browsers covers newer versions of Internet Explorer and Netscape Navigator. This company also provides information to help you select and use search engines.

Consumer Protection Sites

2.1 CONSUMER PROTECTION SITES

The listed websites provide information and services to protect consumers. If you have a problem with an online transaction and are unable to get it resolved, contact one of the services listed for assistance.

Better Business Bureau Online

Website: http://www.bbbonline.org/consumer/complaint.asp

Keywords: Consumer Protection Site (U.S.)

Description: The Better Business Bureau Online is a website where consumers can file complaints about e-commerce sites. It provides information to help consumers reduce unsolicited commercial e-mail, protect personal information, keep passwords private, determine whether a website is legitimate, evaluate business opportunities, protect children online, and understand cookies and privacy. It also provides online shopping tips.

Consumer Sentinel

Website: http://www.consumer.gov/sentinel/index.html

Keywords: Consumer Protection Site (U.S.)

Description: The Consumer Sentinel is a complaint database that provides law enforcement agencies with information on Internet and telemarketing scams. It also monitors other types of fraud-related consumer complaints. You can register complaints at this site.

econsumer.gov

Website: http://www.econsumer.gov/english/index.html

Keywords: Consumer Protection Site (multinational)

Description: Econsumer.gov is a joint effort by 13 countries to combat fraud on the Internet. The website provides information about consumer protection in countries that belong to the IMSN (International Marketing Supervision Network). The site distributes complaints and reports from the Consumer Sentinel's network to IMSN members.

You can report complaints at the website and find information to help you resolve complaints. The site also provides online shopping tips and information on complaint trends.

The Internet Fraud Complaint Center (IFCC)

Website: http://www1.ifccfbi.gov/index.asp

Keywords: Consumer Protection Site

Description: The IFCC is a partnership between the Federal Bureau of Investigation (FBI) and the National White Collar Crime Center (NW3C). The IFCC works to combat fraud committed over the Internet. It operates a central repository for complaints related to the Internet, quantifies fraud patterns, and provides statistical data related to current fraud trends.

You can file complaints related to Internet fraud and find information to help you avoid it.

National Fraud Information Center (NFIC)

Website: http://www.fraud.org/

Keywords: Consumer Protection Site

Description: The NFIC website offers a list of the top ten Internet scams. You can file complaints related to Internet fraud at its website and find information to help you avoid it. It also offers information related to Internet fraud statistics and trends.

National Association of Attorneys General

Website: http://www.naag.org/index.php

Keywords: Attorney General Locator

Description: If you are a victim of consumer fraud on the Web, contact your state Attorney General. Click on *The Attorneys General* link on the top of this page to find contact information.

Marketing Information

3.1 BRAND BUILDING (PRODUCTS & SERVICES)

Brandchannel

Website: http://www.brandchannel.com/start.asp

Keywords: Brand-Related Information and Resources

Description: The Brandchannel website contains information and resources related to branding. The *Books* section contains an extensive list of branding and marketing-related publications with reviews. The *Papers* section features short articles (papers) related to branding and marketing. The *Directory* section lists and describes numerous resources of interest to branding and marketing professionals.

Brand Management (Harcourt College Publishers)

Website: http://www.hbcollege.com/marketing/students/brand.htm

Keywords: Branding-Related Information

Description: The Brand Management website contains assorted information related to branding. The organization's website provides information on branding, brand positioning, brand categories, the key elements of brands, brands and foreign countries, retail branding, private vs. name brands, brand valuation and more.

The brand-related information on this site is good.

Building Brands

Website: http://www.buildingbrands.com/

Keyword: Positioning and Branding Information

Description: BuildingBrands.com features articles in the *Site Archives* section and book reviews in the *Book Reviews* section related to positioning and branding. The positioning book in the book review section by Al Ries and Jack Trout is a great book. It will help you understand the basics of positioning a product or service in the marketplace.

The articles and information offered at this site are interesting and useful.

ClickZ Today

Website: http://www.clickz.com/

Keywords: Brand and Marketing Information

Description: ClickZ has information related to branding, brand marketing, online branding, marketing and more. To find articles, click the arrow on the *Articles by Archive* drop down list and select a subject.

Landor

Website: http://www.landor.com/

Keywords: Branding Dictionary and Articles

Description: Click on the *What is Branding?* link at the top of the page. From the *What is Branding?* page, you can access the Branding Dictionary and branding articles. The articles on this site are good. The Branding Dictionary provides short definitions of common terms related to branding.

3.2 COMPETITIVE INTELLIGENCE

*AuroraWDC.com

Website: http://www.aurorawdc.com/index.htm

Keywords: Competitive Intelligence Information

Description: Click on the *Essays and Articles* link under *Intelligence Resources* in the left column. The page lists various essays and articles to help you develop a competitive intelligence strategy. The articles I reviewed were informative and concise.

CyberAlert

Website: http://www.cyberalert.com/

Keywords: Competitive Intelligence (web monitoring)

Description: CyberAlert provides Internet monitoring and alert services. It offers a variety of service options to help you keep track of competitors. Click the *Product Comparison* link in the left navigation bar to see a detailed comparison of the services.

CyberScan

Website: http://www.clippingservice.com/index.html

Keywords: Competitive Intelligence (web monitoring)

Description: CyberScan provides WebScan and Opinion Monitoring services. Webscan is a service that covers news and information from the WWW. Opinion Monitoring covers usenet newsgroups, listservs, relevant web bulletin boards, and forums. You can purchase the services individually or together. You can also select reporting interval options.

CyberScan services are competitively priced.

eWatch

Website: http://www.ewatch.com/

Keywords: Competitive Intelligence (web monitoring)

Description: eWatch is a service that monitors what consumers, businesses and the media are saying about companies, products, and competitors. eWatch monitors editorial based, public discussion, or other types of websites that you specify. If you need to know what consumers are saying about a product or service online, this is a service worth considering.

Webclipping.com

Website: http://www.webclipping.com/

Keywords: Competitive Intelligence (web monitoring)

Description: Webclipping.com provides Internet monitoring and clipping services. This company will monitor information related to your products and services or those offered by competitors. The cost of its service is reasonable.

3.3 CONSULTING SERVICES

*Marketing Psychology Group

Website: http://www.marketingpsychology.com/index.html

Keywords: Consulting Services, Marketing Information, E-mail Newsletter

Description: The Marketing Psychology Group offers a variety of consulting services and information. The company offers website analysis, website design, website RX, web marketing strategies, advertising and marketing strategies, customer research, general marketing consultations and workshops.

The Marketing Psychology Group approaches marketing problems and concerns in a unique manner. Most people planning a marketing strategy could gain valuable insight from this organization's products and services.

3.4 EMPLOYMENT INFORMATION

Marketingjobs.com

Website: http://www.marketingjobs.com

Keywords: Marketing-Related Job and Salary Information

Description: If you're looking for someone to fill a marketing position or curious about salaries for marketing professionals, this is a good place to start. It's also a good place to go if you're looking for a marketing-related job.

3.5 MARKET ANALYSIS REPORTS

Zapdata.com

Website: http://www.zapdata.com/index.asp

Keywords: Market Analysis Reports by SIC Code

Description: Zapdata is a service offered by Dun & Bradstreet that enables you to get a free market analysis report. If you're marketing a product or service that is defined by an SIC code and need a market analysis report, Zapdata is a good place to start. This is a great site. It has a lot of features and services for individuals or businesses marketing to other businesses.

Standard Industrial Classification (SIC)

3.6 MARKET ANALYSIS (TARGET)

Claritas Express

Website: http://cluster2.claritas.com/ExpressDefault.html (or claritas.com)

Keywords: Target Market Identification and Analysis

Description: Claritas Express offers services to help you identify and reach target groups. Its website is a great resource. Click on the *Free Analysis Tools* link about half way down the page to get an idea of what the firm offers.

Claritas has put a lot of time and thought into its services.

3.7 MARKETING INFORMATION (GENERAL)

*Abraham Group

Website: http://www.abraham.com/Reports.html

Keywords: Marketing and Business Information

Description: This site offers numerous reports related to business and marketing. Click on the *Resources* link on the top of the page to access a list of articles.

You can find numerous reports to help you improve your business and marketing efforts. The information on this site is great.

Action Plan Marketing

Website: http://www.actionplan.com/pdffiles.html

Keywords: Marketing Tips, E-mail Newsletter

Description: The Action Plan Marketing website contains short-but-useful tips to help you develop or revise a marketing strategy. The site is easy to navigate, and the information provided serves as a good review of things that should be considered when developing a marketing strategy.

*All About Marketing

Website: http://www.managementhelp.org/mrktng/mrktng.htm

Keywords: Marketing Information (various topics)

Description: This site is a free community resource used and contributed to by users across the world. There is a vast amount of information on this site related to business, marketing and management. The library was developed by a qualified source. The Management Assistance Program for Nonprofits, in St. Paul, MN, hosts the library.

*The Drayton Bird Partnership

Website: http://www.draytonbird.com/

Keywords: Direct Marketing Information

Description: This site is an excellent source for information related to marketing, direct marketing and direct mail. You'll have to click on one of the birds (top center) to enter the site. To access the information, click on the *277 Answers* link on the bottom of the page or the *Search* link.

*Bpubs.com

Website: http://www.bpubs.com/

Keywords: Marketing and Business Information

Description: Bpubs enables you to search for marketing information and articles. Categories covered include economics, information for entrepreneurs, finance and accounting, human resources, industry publications, intellectual property, Internet and e-commerce, management science, marketing and sales, SOHO and small business.

When you select one of the categories listed above, you are taken to a page with sub-categories.

This site is impressive. It offers a limited amount of information related to marketing. The information and articles offered however, are good.

*Entreprenuer.com

Website: http://www.entrepreneur.com/

Keywords: Marketing Tips (small business)

Description: Entreprenuer.com features useful and practical information for small business owners. Click on the *Marketing* tab near the top of the page to view its marketing-related articles.

This is a good site to visit when you're tiring from information overload. This online publication offers refreshing and informative articles.

HBS Working Knowledge (Harvard Business School)

Website: http://hbswk.hbs.edu/

Keywords: Marketing Articles and Information

Description: Go to the listed address and click on the *Marketing* link in the *Topics* Column. The marketing page contains articles that are interesting and relevant to various types and sizes of businesses. It contains articles related to branding, various aspects of marketing and more.

Iconocast

Website: http://www.iconocast.com/newsletter.html

Keywords: Online Marketing E-mail Newsletter and Archives

Description: Iconocast features a marketing-related e-mail newsletter you can sign up to receive. You can access articles by clicking the *Archive* link at the bottom of the page. The articles on this site are good. I've read many of them, and they're very informative and concise.

Idea Site for Business

Website: http://www.ideasiteforbusiness.com/sitemap.cfm

Keywords: Marketing Information and Tips

Description: This site contains information and tips related to branding, direct mail, direct e-mail brochure design, writing and more. You'll find a variety of marketing information on this site.

Marketing Best Practices

Website: http://www.marketingbestpractices.com/

Keywords: Marketing Articles (small businesses)

Description: Marketing Best Practices contains useful, well-written, concise articles for small businesses. The articles offered contain tips and information to help small businesses market products and services. You can also sign up for a free mini-course for small businesses entitled *Marketing Best Practices*.

To access the articles, go to the listed page and click the *Free Articles* link.

MarketingProfs.com

Website: http://www.marketingprofs.com/index.asp

Keywords: Marketing Information Site

Description: MarketingProfs.com is an online publishing company that specializes in strategic and tactical marketing. Analysts, marketing professionals, and professors often write the articles. The articles I reviewed were well written, concise, and provided useful information.

To access the articles, click the *Archive* tab on the top navigation bar. It takes you to a page where you can access the articles by category.

*MarketingSherpa

Website: http://www.marketingsherpa.com/

Keywords: Marketing Case Studies/Newsletters (e-mail)

Description: The MarketingSherpa offers useful case studies related to Internet and offline marketing. These case studies are of interest to advertising, marketing and PR professionals.

To view the case studies, click on the *Search Library* link at the top of the page. Click on a subject to view a description of the related case studies. Many of the full case studies require a payment. Some of them, however, can be read without paying a fee.

If a listed case study covers what you need to know, it could be money well spent. The prices are reasonable.

You can also sign up for a variety of marketing-related weekly e-mail newsletters.

*Means Business

Website: http://www.meansbusiness.com/default.asp

Keywords: Business Information (aggregated information from published books)

Description: MeansBusiness aggregates information that is handpicked by business editors. This service helps users find the best information from the best books related to a specific subject.

Click a topic in the right column to access a page that lists summaries and related sub-topics. If you see a title or subject that interests you, click on it. You'll be taken to page where you can view short summaries or choose to buy a full summary.

This is a great service. It enables you to find the information you need without having to read numerous books.

Monash University

Website: http://www.buseco.monash.edu.au/depts/Mkt/mtp_online/index.html

Keywords: Marketing Information Site

Description: The Monash University marketing information website contains a lot of information related to marketing theory. The information provided will help you understand various aspects of marketing.

If you have problems finding this page, go to http://www.monash.edu.au/ and click on the *A-Z of Monash Websites* at the bottom of the page. Once you're on the index page, scroll down the alphabetical listings and click on *Marketing, Dept of.*

Small Business Administration (SBA)

Website: http://www.sba.gov/library/pubs.html

Keywords: Business and Marketing Information

Description: The SBA offers a variety of business and marketing information. The organization's website features articles related to Creative Selling, Marketing for Small Businesses, Researching Your Market, Selling by Mail Order, Advertising and Signs, and Showcasing Your Business on the Street.

If you're a small business owner on a limited budget, don't forget to check out the various services that the SBA offers. It offers a variety of services for small businesses.

3.8 MARKETING INFORMATION (MANUFACTURERS)

Harris InfoSource

Website: http://www.harrisinfo.com

Keywords: Manufacturer-Related Marketing Information

Description: Harris InfoSource offers reports and information products of interest to businesses that market to manufacturers. It offers reports related to industry, manufacturing by state and 100 major manufacturing firms.

Harris InfoSource also offers custom lists, databases, and research reports of interest to general business-to-business (BtoB, B2B or BTB) marketers.

3.9 MARKETING PLANNING & STRATEGY

HowStuffWorks

Website: http://biz.howstuffworks.com/marketing-plan2.htm

Keywords: Marketing Plan Information and Guidelines

Description: HowStuffWorks offers useful information to help you develop and understand marketing plans. The information provided gives you a sequential overview of things to consider when developing a marketing plan.

Mplans.com

Website: http://www.mplans.com/

Keywords: Sample Marketing Plans and Software

Description: The Mplans website lets you view sample business plans for various types of businesses. The listed plans were developed with the marketing plan software the site offers. This site is a good place to look for ideas or to compare your marketing plan to one that Mplans has developed. To view all of the plans listed at the site, you'll have to buy its software.

The Marketing Plan Pro software is also listed in the software section of this guide. If you're interested in purchasing planning software, this company's product is worth considering. It's affordable, and the firm has various versions available.

The Write Market

Website: http://www.thewritemarket.com/marketing-plan.shtml

Keywords: Marketing Information, Marketing Plans, Business Planning

Description: The Write Market offers information on a variety of marketing subjects. The *Twenty Ways to Beat Your Competition* is a good reminder of things that can be done to make a product or service stand out.

This site is a good place to review a strategy or look for ideas. The information that is provided on each subject is basic, short and concise. Most small businesses could benefit from one or more of the suggestions offered.

3.10 MARKETING PROJECT COORDINATION

MarketIt Right

Website: http://www.marketitright.com/

Keywords: Marketing Project Coordination and Resources

Description: MarketIt Right is an intermediary service for businesses and marketing-related service providers. The service works to automate marketing communications planning and implementation for businesses.

The services MarketIt Right provides and coordinates are extensive. It streamlines the planning process and brings marketers and service providers together.

3.11 MARKET RESEARCH & INFORMATION

BuyUSA

Website: http://www.buyusa.com/

Keywords: U.S. and International Market Research Reports

Description: The BuyUSA website is operated by the U.S. Department of Commerce. The site contains information related to exporting and U.S. and international market research. You'll have to register to access the international market research section.

eMarketer

Website: http://www.emarketer.com/

Keywords: Internet and E-business Statistics

Description: eMarketer gathers research from over 1,200 sources and makes it available at its website. You'll have to register to use most of its services. If you need statistics related to e-business, this service is worth considering. You can click the *About Us* tab to view the publications offered and see a list of categories at the bottom of the page.

The *Source List* on the *About Us* page (http://www.emarketer.com/about_us/) lists 1,000 research organizations around the world. There's a lot of useful information on this site, but it'll take a few minutes to find it. The reports offered aren't free, but, if they cover what you need to know, they may be well worth the cost.

Forrester Research

Website: http://www.forrester.com/Research/List

Keywords: Technology Trends, Consulting and Information Services

Description: Forrester Research identifies and analyzes trends in technology and their impact on business. This market research firm provides high-end services and reports for companies. Many small businesses will not be able to afford Forrester's products and services.

For large companies or web-related businesses, Forrester Research is a firm to consider. The listed page will help you understand the products and services offered.

Gartner Group

Website: http://www.gartner.com/RecognizedUser

Keywords: Market Research and Market Research Reports

Description: Gartner Group is a market research company that offers research reports related to PCs, servers, workstations, printers, and other computer products. The company also offers reports and research services related to financial services, government, health care, higher education, and small and medium-sized business. Gartner provides custom research services and more.

You can also find worldwide and country-specific reports for numerous industries at its website.

GreenBook

Website: http://www.greenbook.org/

Keywords: Online Research Tools and Services Search Site

Description: Looking for an online research product or service? Go to the listed website and click on the *Online Research Tools and Services* link. The link takes you to a comprehensive guide that lists research services, virtual focus groups, related software, tools and services.

**MarketResearch.com

Website: http://www.marketresearch.com

Keywords: Market Research, Market Research Reports

Description: MarketResearch.com is an excellent place to look for market research reports. This website enables you to search 50,000-plus publications from over 350 leading research firms. You can purchase entire reports or partial reports with its *Buy by the Slice* option.

NPD Intelect

Website: http://www.intelectmt.com/

Keywords: Sales Tracking Services for Electronic Goods and Appliances

Description: If you need to know how and where to sell electronic goods or appliances, NPD Intelect is a good place to start. This company provides sales-tracking services for consumer electronics, home appliances, information technology and imaging-related industries.

Primedia (Business Magazines and Media)

Website: http://www.promomagazine.com/mkt_research.asp

Keywords: Marketing Research Reports and Related Information

Description: The listed page has a search feature that lets you search for targeted research reports from over 250 publishers. You can search for reports related to various countries and industries. The broad categories include business, finance, communications, computers, consumer products, health care, industrial markets, Internet and manufacturing.

Quirk's Marketing Research Review

Website: http://www.quirks.com/

Keywords: Marketing Research Information and Articles

Description: The Quirk's Marketing Research Review website contains articles related to marketing research. Many of the articles cover practical, hands-on approaches to research. Methods used by marketing researchers are the primary focus of the information on this site.

You can search for articles by various criteria in the *Article Archive*.

Quirk's Marketing Research Review also offers a research forum and lists a variety of market research directories.

Researchline

Website: http://library.dialog.com/sourcebook/researchline/

Keywords: Market Research Reports

Description: Researchline contains over 95,000 archived and up-to-date reports from top market research companies. This is a fee service. You can subscribe to it or select an option to pay by credit card.

3.12 MARKETING RESEARCH (TOOLS & RESOURCES)

*ResearchInfo.com

Website: http://www.researchinfo.com/

Keywords: Market Research Forum, Research Software, Web Surveys

Description: Researchinfo.com hosts a market research forum (*The Marketing Research Roundtable*). If you have a question or concern about market research, you might be able to find the answer here. You can also browse the old forum archives.

The site also has a *Research Software Archive*, where you can find trials and demos of software used by market researchers.

The *Web-Survey Tutorial* link will take you to a page with step-by-step instructions to help you create online survey content.

World Opinion

Website: http://www.worldopinion.com/

Keyword: Market Research Resources (global), E-Research Tools

Description: This is a good place to locate market research companies around the world.
The *Directory* tab takes you to a page where you can search for market research companies worldwide.

The *eResearch* link toward the bottom of the left column is another useful page on this site. This page lists a variety of products and services used to do online market research.

3.13 MARKET SEGMENTATION

Abbott Wool's Market Segment Resources

Website: http://www.awool.com/index.html

Keywords: Market Segment Information

Description: The listed website contains information on marketing to African-Americans, Asian-Americans, Hispanics, Teens, Singles, or people 50-plus years of age. It lists resources to reach each of the listed market segments. Listed resources include specialized agencies and media resources that target the listed groups.

Harcourt College Publishers

Website: http://www.harcourtcollege.
com/marketing/students/segmentation.htm

Keywords: Segmentation and Targeting Articles

Description: This page contains a variety of articles related to market segmentation. Areas covered include: segmenting a market, how to identify a target market and prepare a customer profile, niche marketing, specific market segments, pshychographic segmentation and demographic data.

Monash University

Website: http://www.buseco.monash.edu. au/depts/Mkt/mtp_online/mktsegment.html

Keywords: Market Segmentation Information

Description: Monash University offers some useful information on market segmentation. This site is well designed and easy to navigate.

3.14 MARKETING SERVICES (PURCHASING)

BuyersZone.com

Website: http://www.buyerzone.com/index.html

Keywords: Marketing Services (purchasing information)

Description: Buyerszone.com offers information and services to help you purchase marketing services. When you click on a category, you're taken to a page containing information and tips related to purchasing that type of service. The information provided to help you purchase marketing services is the most useful feature of this site.

Buyerzone.com also offers a service that enables you to get multiple quotes from multiple service providers. However, it does not offer comparable information about service providers.

*Elance

Website: http://www.elance.com/

Keywords: Marketing Services (purchasing)

Description: Visit the Elance website and select the *Elance Online* tab to view the services for small businesses. Elance connects buyers and service providers in hundreds of categories. Enter a job description and you'll receive bids from qualified service providers. You can also search for service providers by category and criteria selection.

Elance also offers *Elance Project Services*, which help you with project scoping, vendor selection and/or project management assistance.

3.15 MULTICULTURAL MARKETING

FindArticles.com

Website: http://www.findarticles.com/cf_0/PI/index.jhtml

Keywords: Article Search Tool

Description: FindArticles.com is an excellent place to find specific types of articles. I searched for multicultural marketing information and found an array of articles from leading sources.

FindArticles.com contains articles from more than 300 magazines and journals. You'll find articles related to business, health, society, entertainment, sports and more. You can read entire articles and print them at no cost.

Multicultural Marketing Resources Inc.

Website: http://www.multicultural.com/

Keywords: Multicultural Marketing Information

Description: Multicultural Marketing Resources (MMR) publishes the *Multicultural Mark News* (a paid subscription periodical), *The Source Book of Multicultural Experts* and *MMR e-News* (an online newsletter). MMR is also the host of the *Multicultural Marketing Library and Knowledge Center*, which is available to communication professionals by paid subscription.

The archive section at MMR's site enables you to view information and articles related to multicultural marketing.

3.16 NAMING (BUSINESSES, PRODUCTS, OR SERVICES)

The Naming Newsletter

Website: http://www.namingnewsletter.com/

Keywords: Naming-Related Articles and Newsletters

Description: The Naming Newsletter website contains a variety of interesting and useful articles related to naming.

You can sign up to receive a quarterly update of naming articles offered at this site.

The Naming Workshop

Website: http://www.namingworkshop.com/

Keywords: Naming Workshop (links to related services)

Description: The Naming Workshop offers a service that helps individuals and businesses name a business, product or service. The company also offers a Creating New Names service, which is described at creatingnewnames.com. Neither of these services is cheap, but if you're trying to develop a name for a business, product or service that is going to sell or be sold nationally, or internationally, a good naming strategy is a complex proposition.

3.17 POSITIONING (BUSINESSES, PRODUCTS & SERVICES)

Also see Building Brands (this section)

10 Commandments of Power Positioning

Website: http://www.aniota.com/~jwhite/success1.html

Keywords: Positioning-Related Information

Description: This site contains a ten-part series of information related to positioning products and services. It's good. Unfortunately, if the page is moved, it might be a hard one to find.

If you have problems finding it, try AltaVista's advanced search feature.

3.18 PRESS RELEASE WRITING

Also see Public Relations/Press Releases (this section)

Internet Press Guild

Website: http://www.netpress.org/

Keywords: Press Release Writing Tips

Description: Click on the *Care and Feeding of the Press, a Guide to Sending Out Press Releases* link. You'll be taken to a long and useful article about writing and sending out press releases. It is written from the perspective of public relations professionals. The information contained will help you avoid common mistakes and help you get the most from your press release efforts.

If you have problems finding this page, try http://www.netpress.org/index.html.

PressReleaseWriting.com

Website: http://www.pressreleasewriting.com/

Keywords: Press Release Writing Information and Distribution Services

Description: Need to know more about writing and distributing a press release? This site offers valuable information to help you write a press release. The content basics, ten essential tips, sample press releases and formatting suggestions will help to get you going in the right direction.

Publicity Insider

Website: http://www.publicityinsider.com/index.asp

Keywords: Press Release Writing

Description: The Publicity Insider website contains information to help you write successful press releases. The block of links toward the bottom of the page is the easiest way to access the information on this site.

The information on this site is easy to follow. It covers things you should and should not do in an effective manner.

3.19 PRICING INFORMATION

Professional Pricing Society

Website: http://www.pricingsociety.com/

Keywords: Pricing Information and Resources

Description: The Professional Pricing Societies website contains information and resources related to pricing products and services. Most of the information and resources on this site are of interest to medium-to-large businesses. The top ten pricing books section, however, is one area that would be useful to small business owners.

3.20 PUBLIC RELATIONS/PRESS RELEASES

Automated Press Releases (APR)

Website: http://www.automatedpr.com/index.htm

Keywords: Press Release Writing and Distribution (publications)

Description: Automated Press Releases offers press release writing, editing and distribution services. APR distributes press releases to publications.

The prices of its services are reasonable. APR does not, however, accept credit cards. If you use its services, you'll have to pay for them by check or bank draft.

You can select the type of publications you want your release sent to or leave it up to APR.

*Bacon's (Media Directories)

Website: http://www.bacons.com/

Keywords: Media Directories and Products, Press Release Distribution Services

Description: Bacon's provides a variety of press release distribution services.

The firm also offers media-related publications and products. Its *MediaSource Internet* service lets you search for media resources online. Bacon's also offers *MediaSource Software,* which you install on your system. Both, however, are quality products, and they're relatively priced.

Point to the *Products and Services* link in the top navigation bar to select a product or service to review.

Print Distribution services: The printed press release distribution services here are affordable. They include reproduction of press releases, collating and assembling press kits, direct addressing of envelopes, personalized releases, sample product package assembly, photo and transparency reproduction, special packaging needs, distributing VNRs, sample request fulfillment, hand signing and addressing, merged letters book, and magazine review copy distribution.

Fax Distribution: Bacon's fax press release service addresses releases by name and delivers them in a timely manner.

E-mail Distribution: E-mail Bacon's your press release and it'll do the rest. Upon completion, you'll receive a detailed report of recipients that includes names, titles and telephone numbers.

*Internet News Bureau (INB)

Website: http://www.internetnewsbureau.com/

Keywords: Press Release Services (full-service)

Description: The INB is an established online press release service that enables you to reach more than 10,000 journalists and business professionals. INB will write a press release for you, or edit your release. It'll also post your logo or photo on the INB website. If you have a newsworthy product or service, this service is worth considering.

Market Wire

Website: http://www.marketwire.com/mw/home

Keywords: Press Release Distribution

Description: Market Wire distributes press releases to journalists, analysts, websites, databases, financial information providers and other business professionals. This company provides industry-specific delivery and targeting options in the U.S., Canada and Europe. It also enables you to target specific areas and/or locations. The service enables you to include a logo on press releases.

It's easy to find prices for the various services offered by Market Wire. The *Our Services* link at the bottom of the listed page takes you to a page that describes its services. To access pricing information, scroll to the bottom of this page and click on *click here* under *Our Prices*.

Press Access (LexisNexis)

Website: http://www.pressaccess.com/Default/index.htm

Keywords: Public Relations Resources, Software and Services (high-end)

Description: PressAccess.com features tools and resources for public relations professionals. This firm offers a web-based media relationship management solution, media tracking and contact software, and database of editors and publications. You can register to try various products on a trial basis. The products and services offered are high-end. If you're serious about a public relations campaign, Press Access might have what you need.

The *Free PR Resources* link will help you find hundreds of public relations resources.

*PRWeb

Website: http://www.prweb.com/

Keywords: Free Press Release Service, View Press Releases by Industry

Description: PRWeb lets you view press releases by industry and offers free press release distribution services. Its press release service will post your release at the company's site, make the headlines available to other sites, distribute it through e-mail to filtered recipients and enable it to be indexed by search engines.

This site is operated on a contribution basis. Users that contribute receive upgraded features.

If you need ideas, you can view hundreds of press releases related to specific industries at this site.

3.21 TRADE SHOW INFORMATION

*Trade Show News Network (TSNN)

Website: http://www2.tsnn.com/

Keywords: Trade Show-Related Information and Resources

Description: The TSNN website enables you to search for trade shows and related suppliers. You can also list and search for products and services in various categories. The site gives you access to resources, publications, related associations, international trade show information and more.

There is a vast amount of information, resources and services featured on this site.

*TradeShow Week

Website: http://www.tradeshowweek.com/

Keywords: Trade Show Information, Searches and Related Articles

Description: The TradeShow Week website enables you to search for industry-specific trade shows and related information. Click the *Tradeshow Directory* link to search for industry trade shows around the world.

The *Article Archives* link takes you to a page where you can search for related articles. You can also search for related products and services by clicking the *Buyers Guide* link.

Publications: Tradeshow Week and related directories

3.22 WEB-RELATED MARKETING STATISTICS

eMarketer

Website: http://www.emarketer.com/

Keywords: E-business Statistics and Information (high-end reports)

Description: eMarketer aggregates and analyzes statistics and information from over 1,000 research sources worldwide. The site offers information and reports related to various web industries. It offers a free e-mail newsletter and a variety of information.

3.23 YELLOW PAGE ADVERTISING (AD DESIGN SERVICES)

Ad FX

Website: http://www.ad-fx.com/

Keywords: Yellow Page Ad Design Services and Information

Description: Ad FX specializes in designing yellow page ads. Its website offers a short list of do's and don'ts related to ad design. You can view samples of the firm's work in various categories.

3.24 YELLOW PAGE ADVERTISING (MANAGEMENT SERVICES)

Berry Network

Website: http://www.berrynetwork.com/

Keywords: Yellow Page Advertising Management

Description: If you're placing yellow page ads in numerous directories, a service like this could be helpful. It provides ad placement and related services for larger businesses. It does not serve small accounts of $20,000 or less. Services include: account management, marketing and strategic planning, creative design services, marketing analysis and reporting. This type of service enables you to consistently place ads in multiple directories without having to deal with multiple directory representatives.

Business Information

4.1 BACKGROUND CHECKS

**American Data Bank

Website: http://www.americandatabank.net

Keywords: Background Checks/Business and Personal

Description: American Data Bank does comprehensive background checks of individuals and businesses. The checks include: criminal and civil searches, bankruptcy, lawsuits, etc. This service is an excellent way to find out about a company or individual.

KnowX.com

Website: http://www.knowx.com/

Keywords: Background Checks, Bankruptcy, Reverse Address, Reverse Phone Number, etc.

Description: KnowX.com is an information service that enables you to find information related to individuals and businesses. Many of its services are fee services, but you can try some of them free of charge.

Fee Services Include: background checks, bankruptcy, judgments, liens, lawsuits, UCCs, assets, aircraft, real estate, watercraft and lost money location.

Free Services Include: ultimate people finder, death, divorce, marriage, reverse address, reverse phone number, Internet, 411 directory, professional licenses, ultimate business finder, business yellow pages, corporate records, D&B Business Reports, and more.

4.2 Branding (Business Names)

*Allaboutbranding.com

Website: http://www.allaboutbranding.com/

Keywords: Branding (brand creation, measurement, management, etc.)

Description: If you're trying to create a new brand or work with an existing one, this site has a lot to offer. Its website features insightful articles and useful information to help you create, communicate, measure, manage and extend brands. This site is great. It is well-designed, and the information is good.

*Brandchannel.com (Produced by InterBrand)

Website: http://www.brandchannel.com/start.asp

Keywords: Branding Information, Forum, Books, Papers, etc.

Description: Brandchannel offers a book review section, e-mail newsletter, articles and more. The *Papers* link takes you to the article page, which contains interesting and useful information. The *Books* link takes you to a page that describes books on branding and related subjects. This site is impressive.

NameTrade.com

Website: http://www.nametrade.com/

Keywords: Business Naming and Branding Information

Description: NameTrade.com offers suggestions and information related to selecting a business name. If you're trying to figure out what to do next, or you've run out of ideas, this is a good place to explore. This website contains tips and guidelines to help you understand the name-selection process.

4.3 BUSINESS COUNSELING

Small Business Development Centers

Website: http://www.asbdc-us.org/

Keywords: Business Development Advice and Resources

Description: The Association of Small Business Development Centers website enables you to locate small business development centers. The *Lead Centers* link at the top of the page takes you to a page where you can search for SBDCs by state.

If you're starting a new business or need information about running a business, check to see if there is a SBDC in your area.

*Service Corps of Retired Executives (SCORE)

Website: http://www.score.org/

Keywords: Business Advice and Counseling

Description: SCORE is a program sponsored by the U.S. Small Business Administration to assist small businesses. Score has 10,500 volunteer business counselors that provide small business mentoring and advice. You can get advice via e-mail or in person.

4.4 BUSINESS INFORMATION (GENERAL)

*Ask an Expert

Website: http://www.libraryspot.com/askanexpert.htm

Keywords: Questions or Problems? Ask an Expert Volunteer

Description: This site lists hundreds of professionals and volunteers willing to answer questions. If you need an answer to a question and don't know whom to ask, this site is a good place to start.

*Bpubs.com

Website: http://www.bpubs.com/

Keywords: Business Information

Description: Bpubs enables you to search for business information and articles. Categories covered include economics, entrepreneur, finance and accounting, human resources, industry publications, intellectual property, Internet and e-commerce, management science, marketing and sales, SOHO and small business.

When you select one of the categories listed above, you are taken to a page with sub-categories.

This site is impressive. The information and articles that you can access from this site are good. You can find a lot of useful and relevant information easily.

Business Courseware

Website: http://newarkwww.rutgers.edu/guides/business/

Keywords: Business and Marketing Information

Description: The Business Courseware website provides information and resources in a convenient, click-through sequence. When you click on a category, you're taken to a page with relevant subject matter and additional links.

Main categories offered: business planning, company research, financial analysis, product research and international business research.

*Business Owners' Idea Café

Website: http://www.businessownersideacafe.com/

Keywords: Business Information (general-small business)

Description: The Business Owners' Idea Café offers useful information for small businesses. The site has pages dedicated to starting a business, business grants, business planning, running a business, marketing, financing, human resources, etc.

Each section of this site has a forum where you can post questions or view the answers to questions already posted. To find the various sections, scroll to the bottom of the page until you see the block of navigation links.

This is a great site for small business owners. It has some great content and features. A lot of thoughtful hard work and talent went into this site.

eLibrary

Website: http://ask.elibrary.com/index.asp

Keywords: General Information Searches (magazines, newspapers)

Description: eLibrary enables you to search hundreds of sources for articles related to specific subjects. Type in the subject and the descriptions of related articles are displayed. When you click on an article, you'll be shown a portion of the article. To read the full article, you'll have to sign up for a trial membership or become a member.

Depending on the information you're looking for, this could be a valuable service. It would work for monitoring competitor press releases, keeping up on industry-related news and more.

*FindArticles.com

Website: http://www.findarticles.com/cf_0/PI/index.jhtml

Keywords: Article Search Tool

Description: FindArticles.com is an excellent place to find specific types of articles. You can use it to search for various articles from an array of sources. It's a great service.

FIND SVP

Website: http://www.findsvp.com/default.cfm

Keywords: Knowledge Services Company

Description: Find SVP is a knowledge services company that offers a broad range of marketing services. Its one-time question answering option might be a service that saves the day. For $250, the company will spend three hours finding an answer to a tough question. If you have a question or problem and can't find an answer anywhere else, this service is worth considering.

*Free Management Library

Website: http://www.managementhelp.org

Keywords: General Advertising, Marketing and Management Tips

Description: This site offers good advertising, marketing and business information. If you're developing a marketing or advertising strategy, this site is worth visiting. The information is presented in a manner that reminds you of important things to consider.

This site is listed more than once in this guide, because it is broad and useful.

Infomine

Website: http://infomine.ucr.edu/

Keywords: Internet Information Sources (general)

Description: Infomine is a virtual library of Internet resources. The information and resources you can access from this site are extensive.

*Means Business

Website: http://www.meansbusiness.com/default.asp

Keywords: Business Information (aggregated information)

Description: MeansBusiness aggregates information that is hand picked by business editors. The service helps users find the best information from the best books related to specific subjects.

Example: If you follow links to the *Strategic Plan Implementation* page on this site, you will see a brief quote from nine chosen sources. For $9, you can buy the extracts available at the site. What you end up with is relevant information selected from nine published sources.

4.5 BUSINESS INFORMATION (INDUSTRY SPECIFIC)

Online-pr.com

Website: http://www.online-pr.com/

Keywords: Industry Specific Sites

Description: The sites you can access from this page are good. It is a good starting point to locate websites that offer industry-specific information.

Saint Joseph's University

Website: http://www.sju.edu/

Keywords: Food and Beverage Marketing Library

Description: The SJU Academy of Food Marketing website has information and resources related to marketing food and beverages. It contains the following categories: *Association/Organizations*, *E-publications*, *Government Links*, *New Books List*, *Periodicals in Print* and a notable *Where to Find* page.

The *Where to Find* link takes you to a page with resources commonly used by food and beverage marketers.

To find this page, go to http://www.sju.edu/ and click on the *Library* link at the top of the page. The library page contains a link for the *Food Marketing Library*.

The URL for the *Food Marketing Library* is listed below. It is however, an extended address, which commonly change.

http://www.sju.edu/hsb/campbell/pages/where.htm#d

Software Marketing Resources

Website: http://www.softwaremarketingresource.com/

Keywords: Software Marketing Information

Description: The SMR website contains resources for software developers, publishers and user groups.

Buyers Guides: The *Buyers Guides* section contains links to industry-specific buyers guides.

Software Sites: The *Software Sites* section takes you to a page that lists numerous software-related websites. This page is an excellent place to look for freeware, shareware and software publisher websites.

4.6 BUSINESS INFORMATION (NEW BUSINESSES)

Zeromillion.com, Inc.

Website: http://www.zeromillion.com/

Keywords: Business Articles (basic-intermediate, entrepreneurs)

Description: ZeroMillion.com contains articles of interest to anyone starting or running a business. The articles and information on this site are easy to find and read. Information for new business owners is the primary focus.

If you're starting a business or need a review of what's involved, there is a lot of useful information on this site. It is a great site. It is well-organized and easy to use.

4.7 BUSINESS INTELLIGENCE

Cyveillance, Inc.

Website: http://www.cyveillance.com/

Keywords: Business Intelligence Services (high-end, online)

Description: Cyveillance, Inc. is a leading provider of e-business intelligence services. The services include brand management, partner management, digital asset protection, corporate security, competitive intelligence and custom data mining.

Cyveillance provides highly relevant intelligence services for businesses. Its services help businesses recapture revenue, reduce costs, improve operational efficiencies and more.

4.8 BUSINESS PLANS & RELATED INFORMATION

Bplans.com

Website: http://www.bplans.com/

Keywords: Business, Marketing, Advertising, and Website Plans

Description: Bplans.com has a variety of business, marketing, advertising and website plans you can review. The listed page has links to pages that list the various types of plans.
If you're looking for ideas or you want to compare your plan to others, this might be a good place to start.

Also, see Marketing Plans in the Marketing Information Section: Many of the sites that offer information about marketing plans provide information on business planning also.

Center for Business Planning

Website: http://www.businessplans.org/

Keywords: Business Plan Evaluation

Description: The Center for Business Planning (CBP) offers Strategy Insight, which is a service that evaluates business plans. Strategy Insight asks you to answer a series of questions, which are analyzed. The analysis produces information related to market position, potential for success, potential problems and tests alternatives. Strategy Insight is an affordable service.

CBP also offers software, resources and sample business plans. It offers software to help you with business, strategic and marketing plans. You'll also find software to help you determine market demand, and develop marketing, pricing and sales strategies.

*HowStuffWorks

Website: http://www.howstuffworks.com/

Keywords: Business Planning, Online Business Planning, Selling, etc,

Description: HowStuffWorks is an information site that contains information on business planning, marketing, selling, customer service and more. This site is listed more than once in this directory because of its forward and effective approach to providing useful information. There is a lot of valuable and useful information on this site.

To access the business information page, type *business* in the search box at the top of the page.

Startup Journal (wsj.com)

Website: http://wsj.miniplan.com/

Keywords: Business Planning Service

Description: The Startup Journal is operated by the Wall Street Journal. This site has a business-planning feature that you can use to develop a business plan. Privacy, however, is something you might want to consider before using this service. Do you want to use a public service to develop your business plan?

4.9 BUSINESS PRODUCTS (LOCATING)

Hoover's Solution Center

Website: http://hoovers.knowledgestorm.com

Keywords: IT Product and Service Selection (excellent site)

Description: Hoover's Solution Center is an excellent place to search for information technology (IT) solutions. You can search for business applications, industry-specific applications, IT services, web development tools and applications, and infrastructure and system management tools.

To get an overview of the products and service listed, click on the *Browse Complete Directory* link at the bottom of the page.

Thomas Register

Website: http://www.thomasregister.com/

Keywords: Business Products, Packaging, Display Racks, Boxes, etc.

Description: The Thomas Register website is an excellent place to search for thousands of items. You can also find this publication in print form at most libraries. Its website is great. You can use it to locate suppliers and manufacturers of hundreds of types of items.

4.10 BUYERS GUIDES

Software Marketing Resources

Website: http://www.softwaremarketingresource.com/

Keywords: Links to Industry-Specific Buyers Guides

Description: Click on the *Click Here* link toward the bottom, left-hand corner to enter the site. The *Buyers Guides* link in the left navigation bar takes you to a page that has links for industry-specific buyers guides. This site is a good place to start if you're looking for industry-specific products and services.

4.11 COMPETITIVE INTELLIGENCE (ONLINE)

eWatch

Website: http://www.ewatch.com/

Keywords: Competitive Intelligence

Description: eWatch is a service that monitors what consumers, businesses and the media are saying about companies, products, and competitors. eWatch monitors editorial-based, public discussion, and any other type of website requested. If you need to know what consumers are saying about a product or service online, this is a service worth considering.

4.12 CONSULTING SERVICES

Find/SVP

Website: http://www.findsvp.com/

Keywords: Consulting Services

Description: Find/SVP is a service that provides information and consulting services. The resources and services it offers are substantial. Its services aren't cheap, but, if you really need to know something, they're worth considering.

4.13 COPYRIGHTS

Copyright Website

Website: http://www.benedict.com/default.asp

Keywords: Copyright Information

Description: The Copyright Website provides information related to copyrights.

Copyright Clearance Center, Inc.

Website: http://www.copyright.com/CopyrightResources/default.asp

Keywords: Copyright Information

Description: The Copyright Clearance Center, Inc. is the largest licenser of text reproduction rights in the world. CCC provides licensing systems for the reproduction and distribution of copyrighted materials in print and electronic formats. Its website contains useful information related to copyright laws.

4.14 DISPLAY AND MERCHANDISING PRODUCTS

Creative (The Magazine of Promotion and Marketing)

Website: http://www.creativemag.com/homepage.html

Keywords: Point of Purchase Displays, Trade Show Exhibits, etc.

Description: The Creative website contains hundreds of listings related to displays, racks, and merchandising hardware. If you're operating a physical store, this site lists numerous products and services that may be of interest.

The *Advertiser Index* tab at the top of the page takes you to a page that lists companies advertising in the publication. You can search for specific product types by clicking the link at the top of the page that enables you to search by category.

Point of Purchase (Retail Magazine)

Website: http://www.popmag.com/pointofpurchase/index.jsp

Keywords: Point of Purchase Buyers Guide

Description: The POP website contains a POP Online Buyers Guide, which is a comprehensive resource of POP solutions for retailers. To access it, click on the *Buyers Guide* link in the left navigation box.

4.15 DOMAIN NAMES & TRADEMARKS

The Internet Corporation for Assigned Names & Numbers (ICANN)

Website: http://www.icann.org/

Keywords: Central Naming Authority (accredited registrars and information)

Description: ICANN is the non-profit corporation that was formed to assume responsibility for Internet names. The organization is responsible for IP address space allocation, protocol parameter assignment, domain name system management, and root server system management functions previously performed under U.S. Government contract by IANA and other entities.

You can find a list of accredited registrars at the ICANN site. You can also report complaints about registrars.

Its website features a variety of information related to Internet naming.

International Trademark Association (INTA)

Website: http://www.inta.org/

Keywords: International Trademark Information

Description: The INTA website provides information related to international trademarks. The *TM Basics* page contains links to pages related to: Frequently Asked Questions, Fact Sheets, Feature Articles, Trademark Links and a Trademark Glossary.

The *Site Map* provides a good overview of the INTA site.

It offers an e-mail discussion list to help users find answers to trademark-related questions (requires registration). The list provides a forum for the exchange of trademark-related questions and related ideas. It has over 1,800 subscribers.

Network Solutions

Website: http://www.networksolutions.com/en_US/index.jhtml

Keywords: Domain Name Registrar

Description: Network Solutions is an established name registrar. It has been around for a long time. You can find better prices but I don't know if you can find a better service. I've never had a name expire through this service without receiving multiple e-mail and postal notifications.

RegistarStats

Website: http://www.registrarstats.com/

Keywords: Internet Registrar Statistics

Description: Trying to decide on a registrar for your domain names? This site features information to help you select a name registrar. It's a great website.

Startup Journal (wsj.com)

Website: http://wsj.miniplan.com/

Keywords: Trademark Searches

Description: The Startup Journal offers a trademark search feature on its website. Go to the listed page and click on the *Trademark Search* link in the left sidebar. You can perform searches for Federal, Canadian and European Trademarks. It also searches for domain names.

TradeName.com

Website: http://www.tradename.com/

Keywords: U.S. and International Trademark Information and Resources

Description: Tradename.com is an e-commerce intellectual property service. It offers worldwide trademark-related services. The services offered include searches, registrations, assignments, and management. Its website contains useful links, a questions and answers section and other useful information.

U.S. Patent & Trademark Office

Website: http://www.uspto.gov/

Keywords: Trademark Search and Registration Site

Description: The U.S. Patent and Trademark office contains a lot of useful information to help you select and register a trademark. The search function on this site enables you to search for federally registered Trademarks.

4.16 DROP SHIPPING

Also see Order Fulfillment and Warehousing (this section)

Drop Shipping News

Website: http://www.drop-shipping-news.com/

Keywords: Drop Shipping Information

Description: The Drop Shipping News website lists drop-shipping-related publications and articles you can order. The information products offered at this site are affordable.

Publications Offered:
Drop Shipping Source Directory of Major Consumer Product Lines
Drop Shipping Marketing Methods
Drop Shipping as a Marketing Function, a Handbook of Methods and Policies
Consumer Products Source Directory

4.17 GOVERNMENT CONTRACTS

Onvia

Website: http://www.onvia.com/

Keywords: Government Contract Information Service (Fee Service)

Description: Onvia is an information service that keeps businesses informed about products and services that various government agencies are interested in purchasing. When you sign up for this service, you will be informed when an agency is interested in purchasing the type of product or service you offer.

4.18 ORDER FULFILLMENT & WAREHOUSING

Drop Ship Express

Website: http://www.dropshipexpress.com/index.html

Keywords: Order Fulfillment, Drop Shipping

Description: Drop Ship Express (DSE) offers an array of services for businesses of every size. Distribution and warehousing services similar to those offered by DSE have become very popular. DSE allows businesses to concentrate on producing and selling products without the fixed costs of dedicated warehousing and shipping facilities.

DSE has warehousing and shipping centers strategically located to reduce mailing costs.

iFulfill

Website: http://www.ifulfill.com/

Keywords: Full-Service Fulfillment Services

Description: iFulfill provides full-service fulfillment services for web merchants. Click on the *Check us Out* link in the upper left hand corner of the listed page. The link takes you to a page that explains the services.

iFulfill offers a complete service option for small web businesses. This option includes product warehousing, a secure shopping cart, credit card processing, and picking, packing, shipping, tracing and tracking orders.

The firm also offers other options to suit the different needs of web business owners.

iFulfillment

Website: http://www.ifulfillment.com/index.html

Keywords: Order Fulfillment Service (e-commerce)

Description: iFulfillment is a leading provider of order fulfillment services. If you're selling products directly from a website, you might want to consider a service like this to handle warehousing, shipping, returns and order processing. iFulfillment provides fulfillment services for leading companies. iFulfillment can also take on high-volume accounts.

Netship

Website: http://www.netship.com/index.html

Keywords: Order Fulfillment Service (e-commerce)

Description: Netship offers order fulfillment and inventory services for small-to-medium-sized businesses via the Internet. It operates inventory locations throughout the U.S., and provides domestic and import distribution as well as auction seller services.

4.19 PRICING

Professional Pricing Society

Website: http://www.pricingsociety.com

Keywords: Pricing Information

Description: Wondering what to charge for products or services? The Professional Pricing Society's website features an array of information and products to help businesses price products and services.

4.20 SHIPPING INFORMATION & TRACKING

Accuship

Website: http://www.accuship.com/

Keywords: Shipping Logistics Solutions

Description: Accuship provides advanced shipping logistics solutions for businesses. The solutions provided by Accuship are medium to high-end. If you are a volume shipper, you might want to consider one of its solutions.

Federal Express

Website: http://www.fedex.com/us/

Keywords: Federal Express Shipping and Tracking Information

Description: The Federal Express website enables you to find information related to its services. You can find pricing information, track packages, request pickups and more.

*iShip

Website: http://www.iship.com/default.htm

Keywords: Shipping Selection and Pricing Tool (up to 150 lbs.)

Description: iShip provides information related to multi-carrier shipping services. Select the weight, origin and destination of a package and iShip will calculate the rates charged by various services.

You can compare rates and services provided by UPS, DHL, FedEx Express, FedEx Ground, Airborne Express and the U.S. Postal Service.

InterShipper

Website: http://www.intershipper.com/

Keywords: Shipping Selection Tool (up to 150 lbs.)

Description: Intershipper is a service that enables you to price, select, track, and organize the shipment of packages. Type in the weight, origin, and destination and you'll know how much common shipping services charge for various levels of service.

InterShipper is a great service. It provides shippers with useful information quickly.

Pack Track

Website: http://www.packtrack.com/

Keywords: Package Tracking Site

Description: Pack Track enables you to track items shipped through multiple shippers. Enter a tracking number and select the shipper and Pack Track will locate the item. You'll have to register to use this service.

United Parcel Service (UPS)

Website: http://www.ups.com/index.html

Keywords: UPS Service Information

Description: The UPS website enables you to track packages, locate drop off points, order supplies, request pick-up, look up rates, etc.

4.21 SHIPPING SERVICES (HEAVY FREIGHT)

Also see Shipping Information & Tracking (this section)
Drop-Shipping (this section)

Air-Pac

Website: http://www.freightforwarders.org/

Keywords: International Freight and Forwarder Service

Description: Air-Pac Freight Carrier is a global trucking company that provides international freight services.

Freightquote.com

Website: http://www.freightquote.com/

Keywords: Service Provider Selection and Coordination

Description: Freightquote offers a service that enables business-to-business customers to view the offerings of multiple carriers. This service covers less-than-truckload, truckload, expedited, local cartage and intermodal freight.

Freight World

Website: http://www.freightworld.com/

Keywords: Shipping Information and Services Portal

Description: Freightworld.com is a shipping information and resource portal. If you need to plan or evaluate a shipment of goods, this is a good place to start. The *Logistics Providers* link will take you to a page where you can find a service to manage the process.

The information and resources on this site will enable you to ship about anything anywhere.

ShippingFinder.com

Website: http://www.shippingfinder.com/

Keywords: Shipping Intermediary Website

Description: ShippingFinder.com enables you to post a shipping request and receive bids from multiple service providers. The services offered are free to shippers. The service provider pays for this service.

The primary service provided by ShippingFinder.com is to bring shippers and shipping companies together. After the shipper and shipping company complete a deal, the account is settled between them, not by ShippingFinder.com.

4.22 SUPPLY CHAIN MANAGEMENT

Industrial Data & Information (IDII)

Website: http://www.idii.com/home.htm

Keywords: Supply Chain Software, Newsletter, Information and Resources

Description: If you're looking for information related to supply chain management software, this is good place to start. Its website contains a substantial amount of information related to software used to manage supply chain operations.

4.23 TRADEMARKS

See Domain Names & Trademarks (this section)

Business Information

5.1 BUSINESS & CONSUMER LISTS (DIRECT MARKETING)

AccuData

Website: http://www.accudata.com/

Keywords: Mailing and Marketing Lists (business and consumer)

Description: AccuData offers an assortment of data services for all types of consumer and business-to-business marketers. Its website features an array resources and information to help direct marketers succeed. It is well designed and it's easy to find what you're looking for.

Direct Media

Website: http://www.directmedia.com/index.htm

Keywords: Mailing and Marketing Lists

Description: Select the *Direct Mail* link in the left column. Then select *Managed Lists* from the drop down list to view the lists offered. Its website contains a lot of useful information and resources for direct marketers.

GreatLists.com

Website: http://www.greatlists.com/

Keywords: Business Lists (postal, e-mail, telephone, fax)

Description: Great Lists offers a variety of lists for individuals and businesses interested in marketing to businesses. It can provide lists of subscribers to business-related publications. The firm also has a database of 12 million U.S. businesses from which you can have a custom list created by selecting variables.

Harris InfoSource

Website: http://www.harrisinfo.com

Keywords: Business Sales and Marketing Lists (businesses and manufacturers)

Description: Harris InfoSource provides sales and marketing information to help businesses market to other businesses. It offers reference directories, databases, research reports, case studies and lists. Harris InfoSource's directories and products are business-to-business oriented. This firm has a lot of useful information for any company that wants to market to manufacturers.

InfoUSA.com

Website: http://www.databaseamerica.com/

Keywords: Business Sales Leads, Mailing Lists, Credit Reports, etc.

Description: InfoUSA offers business sales leads and mailing lists, customer analyzing and prospect building services, business credit reports, and sales and marketing directories in print and CD-ROM.

ListBank

Website: http://www.listbank.com/

Keywords: Business and Consumer Lists (domestic and international)

Description: ListBank offers a wide selection of business and consumer lists.

Think Direct Marketing.com

Website: http://www.thinkdirectmarketing.com/splashpgs/usps.htm

Keywords: Subscription-Based Consumer and Business Marketing Lists

Description: Think Direct Marketing is an authorized affiliate merchant of the USPS. Think Direct Marketing offers subscription-based marketing lists. A yearly fee enables you to access up to 20,000 business or consumer prospects. There are no per name or per usage fees.

Vanguard Publishing Company

Website: http://www.thebizadvantage.com/index.html

Keywords: Business Lists, Marketing Directories, etc.

Description: Vanguard Publishing offers regional business and marketing directories, custom business-to-business mailing lists, top U.S. company lists, an employers directory and job search engine, and contact software.

The data offered is available in different formats to suit your specific needs.

5.2 BUSINESS & CONSUMER LIST SELECTION (MARKETING)

American List Counsel (ALC)

Website: http://search.alcdata.com/market

Keywords: Business and Consumer List Selection

Description: The ALC website enables you to search for a direct mail or marketing list by various criteria. You can search by media, sector, geography, list universe, average unit of sale and more.

SRDS Media Solutions

Website: http://www.srds.com/

Keywords: List Selection Information and Services

Description: Go to the SRDS website and select the *Subscription and Product Information* link. From there, scroll down until you see the *Direct Marketing* links in the right navigation column. SRDS offers a Direct Marketing List Source and SRDS DirectNet service to help you select the right list. The company's services aren't cheap but if you're serious about a direct marketing campaign, it may be money well spent.

5.3 BUSINESS DIRECTORIES

Thomas Global Register

Website: http://www.aernet.com/

Keywords: Global Directory of Manufacturers and Distributors

Description: The Thomas Global Register is a directory of 500,000 manufacturers and distributors from 22 countries. It enables you to find suppliers in foreign markets and related information.

5.4 DATABASE SERVICES (BUSINESS & CONSUMER)

Marketing Software Company

Website: http://www.mscnet.com/index.htm

Keywords: Database Services (high-end business and consumer)

Description: MSC offers database services that include data from different databases. It has the data and expertise to create custom marketing data. If you want to create or improve a list for a large marketing campaign, this service is worth considering.

The firm also offers information on geographic entities, statistics, Hispanic surname identification, file enhancements and mapping information services.

5.5 INFORMATION ABOUT BUSINESSES

Big Book

Website: http://www.bigbook.com/

Keywords: Directory Information

Description: This site is a good place to locate a business or organization. I used it to find several businesses throughout the U.S. The listings came up quick and were accurate.

CorpTech

Website: http://www.corptech.com/

Keywords: High-tech Company Information (50,000-plus)

Description: CorpTech publishes data on high-tech manufacturing, development and related services. Its listings include companies that offer products and services related to computers, lasers, biotech products, advanced materials and hundreds of other categories. You can purchase individual company reports on a pay-per-view basis. You can also purchase lists of companies by industry, region or state.

You can sign up for a free guest membership to preview its services. The company also offers a variety of subscription options.

Dun & Bradstreet

Website: http://www.dnb.com

Keywords: Credit Information and Reports (business)

Description: Dun & Bradstreet offers credit reports for businesses, marketing lists of businesses with appropriate credit ratings, collection services, a tracking folder service that enables you to keep track of a company's credit rating, and supplier search services.

The tracking folder services offered enable you to monitor the credit rating of your business or other businesses. At the time of this writing, Dun & Bradstreet's folder service enabled a company to monitor its credit and the credit of up to 14 suppliers. If the credit rating of any of the entered companies changes, the registrar would be notified of the changes. Dun & Bradstreet's folder service is a great service for businesses that need or want to monitor the financial integrity of their suppliers, and/or partners.

Credit Reports: If you need credit information related to a specific company, you can look it up on its website and order a report.

Factiva

Website: http://www.factiva.com/

Keywords: Company-Specific Business News and Information

Description: Factiva is a news delivery service operated by Dow Jones and Reuters. It is a subscription service that delivers company-specific, industry-specific, and general business news via the web.

This service is useful to keep track of company-specific press releases, news, trade articles, etc. If you need to keep up on business or industry-specific news, this is a service worth considering. The service will cost you but it is a good way to get relative information and news fast.

Hoover's Business Press

Website: http://www.hoovers.com

Keywords: Business Directories (specific high-end)

Description: Hoover's offers business reference publications that provide information on American business, world business, emerging companies, private companies and international companies.

International Guides: Brazil Company Handbook, Canadian Company Information, Germany's Top 500, Japan Company Handbook, and the Trade Directory of Mexico.

Business Resource Directories: Association Directories, County and City Data Book, Headquarters USA, Statistical Abstract of the United States.

Industry Guides: computers and Internet, energy, entertainment and media, engineering and research, finance and investments, health care and biotech.

Infobel.com

Website: http://www.infobel.com/teldir/

Keywords: National and International Telephone Directories

Description: Infobel is an index of online telephone directories. It enables you to access yellow pages, white pages and business directories for over 184 countries.

LLRX.com

Website: http://www.llrx.com/index.htm

Keywords: Business Research Information

Description: LLRX.com provides up to date information on a wide range of Internet research tools and resources. The information and resources on this site are vast. If you need to know how to find something on the Internet, this website is a good place to start.

To access the research links, you can scroll down and click on the *LawPro Links* in the left navigation column. The LawPro Links page contains links to resources that enable you to research companies and more.

OneSource Information Services, Inc.

Website: http://www.onesource.com/index.htm

Keywords: Company-Specific Reports

Description: OneSource provides information related to public and private companies. Its Business Browser product line provides business and financial information on over one million public and private companies. Its services are web-based.

5.6 LIST PROCESSING SERVICES

Marketing Software Company (MSC)

Keywords: List Processing Services (high-end)

Website: http://www.mscnet.com/prodserv/index.htm

Description: MSC offers file conversions, address standardization and zip code correction, national change of address, customized list services, obscenity scanning, country name standardization, title standardization, duplicate elimination, segmentation/key coding, on line counts, gender counts, personalized salutations, upper/lower casing, postal pre-sorting, output options and data entry services.

MSC programmers are capable of taking on complex list projects.

NationalChangeofAddress.com

Website: http://www.nationalchangeofaddress.com/

Keywords: Address List Processing Services

Description: National Change of Address.com is a service that provides NCOA list processing. NCOA is a process that matches a file of names and addresses to the United States Postal Service licensed NCOA database, which is comprised of more than 106 million records of individual, family and business moves. Nationalchangeofaddress.com is not a U.S. Postal Service website.

The FAQs link at the top of the listed web pages takes you to a page that will help you understand the services offered and why your list might need updating.

(NCOA) National Change of Address

Advertising

6.1 AD DESIGN

AdBusters

Website: http://www.adbusters.org/home/

Keywords: Ad Design Examples and Information, Magazine

Description: AdBusters is a unique site. The entire site reflects an in depth perspective of ad design. The *Info* link at the top of the page will take you to an information page. Click *Search the Site* on the information page and you'll be taken to a page where you can search for information related to ad design. I performed a search for *ad design tips* and found useful articles related to ad design.

This site contains and enormous amount of information. Most of it is related to the creative thinking behind ad design. There is, however, some practical and useful information.

AdCracker

Website: http://www.adcracker.com/

Keywords: Ad Design and Copy Writing, Tips and Interactive CD

Description: The AdCracker website features AdBasics, AdCreative and AdManagement pages that contain ad-related tips and information. This site features some interesting content. It is a great place to stimulate creativity.

The AdCracker CD is a tool to help you design ads, write copy for ads and manage advertising and marketing-related activities.

6.2 ADVERTISING GLOSSARY

Interactive Advertising Bureau

Website: http://www.iab.net/resources/glossary.asp

Keywords: Glossary of Interactive Advertising Terms

Description: The IAB website has features that enable you to search for definitions and abbreviations related to web and interactive advertising.

6.3 ADVERTISING INFORMATION

AdForum

Website: http://www.adforum.com/

Keywords: Advertising Information Portal

Description: AdForum is an advertising portal with information and links for advertisers. Its website is a good place to search for advertising firms, production companies and directors, and creative resources.

For an overview of the sites contents, click the *Site Map* link at the bottom of the page.

*Advertising and Promotion

Website: http://www.managementhelp.org

Keywords: General Advertising and Marketing Tips

Description: Go to the listed page and click on *Advertising and Promotion.*

This website is a great place to look for advertising information. The information is easy to find and good. You can access information related to advertising basics, preparation, evaluation, general resources, advertising law, writing ads, direct mail, mailing lists, signs and displays, classified advertising, radio and TV, online advertising and promotion, measuring results and more.

This site is listed more than once in this guide because it is broad and useful.

6.4 ADVERTISING AND MARKETING LAWS

ADLAW

Website: http://www.adlaw.com/rc/index.html

Keywords: Legal Issues Related to Advertising and Marketing

Description: ADLAW features legal information related to sweepstakes, cyber-marketing, advertising, marketing, contract forms and more. The *ADLAW Handbook* link takes you to a page that covers legal issues related to advertising, marketing and related subjects.

Advertising Law Resource Center

Website: http://www.lawpublish.com/

Keywords: Advertising Law and Related Information

Description: The Advertising Law Resource Center's website contains links to articles and information for advertisers. A few of the links provide useful information about advertising specific types of products.

Federal Trade Commission (FTC)

Website: http://www.ftc.gov/ftc/business.htm

Keywords: Advertising and Business Information

Description: The *Business Publications* link takes you to a page with a subject list. Click on a subject to view related titles. There is a lot of useful information related to advertising, doing business online and other subjects. You will also find information to help you avoid problems associated with improper advertising and marketing techniques.

Global Advertising Lawyers Alliance (GALA)

Website: http://www.gala-marketlaw.com/

Keywords: Laws and Legal Issues, International Advertising and Marketing

Description: The GALA website enables you to research legal issues and laws related to advertising in foreign countries. Each country link lists advertising lawyers. Many feature a country report link you can click to review laws related to advertising in the country.

The laws or restrictions of some countries limit the information that can be posted.

Write101.com

Website: http://www.write101.com/

Keywords: Advertising and Writing-Related Articles

Description: Write101.com contains numerous articles related to advertising and small business issues. Go to the listed page and scroll ½ way down the page. Click on the *Advertising Tips* link in the left column. Many of the articles on this site are great. They're short and concise.

Click on the *Archive Link* in the top navigation bar to view articles related to various aspects of writing.

6.5 ADVERTISING PLACEMENT LOCATOR

Also see Media Search (this section)

Ad Base

Website: http://www.adbase.net/

Keywords: Website Ad Placement Search Database

Description: Ad Base is a database service that enables you to search for websites to place advertising on. Searches are performed by category. This is also good place to list your site if you want to accept advertising.

If you select a site to advertise on from this site, consider two things. How you will be charged and how you'll know what you're getting for you're money.

Banner Ad Placement Study

Website: http://webreference.com/dev/banners/

Keywords: Banner Ad Placement Study (page orientation)

Description: The studies on this page relate to the effectiveness of banner ads placed on different areas of a web page. The studies concluded that banners placed in the lower-right corner of a page, or 1/3 of the way down, outperformed top-placement. These studies are old, but they're worth considering.

Electronic Journal Miner

Website: http://ejournal.coalliance.org/

Keywords: Electronic Publication Search

Description: The Electronic Journal Miner's website is a good place to search for e-mail periodicals and other electronic publications. It lists thousands of electronic periodicals related to thousands of subjects.

This site is an excellent place to find highly specialized electronic periodicals to advertise in or subscribe to.

eMediaReport

Website: http://www.emediaresources.com/

Keywords: Website Advertising Placement Strategy

Description: eMediaReport is a service that uses a database-driven research system to locate your target market. Its profiles include website synopsis (comprehensive view), demographic/geographic information, advertising and marketing opportunities, targeting abilities, contact information and more.

This service can help you gain an understanding of your competition, develop a marketing strategy, locate industry-specific websites, directories, and more.

6.6 AD VIEWING

AdFlip

Website: http://www.adflip.com/

Keywords: Ad Preview Site

Description: Ad Flip contains hundreds of ads you can preview. This is an excellent site to visit if you need to get an idea of what other companies are doing. To access all the features, you'll have to join. You can sign up for one week or longer.

6.7 BANNER ADS (SAMPLES)

Banner Ad Museum

Website: http://www.banneradmuseum.com/Mission.html

Keywords: Banner Ad Samples

Description: The Banner Ad Museum is a repository of banner ads organized by business type and country. If you want to see what other businesses are doing with banner ads, this is a good place to start.

To view the ads, you can scroll down on the listed page and click on the *Galleries* icon.

6.8 E-MAIL AND EZINE ADVERTISING

LifeMinders

Website: http://www.lifeminders.com

Keywords: E-mail Advertising Service

Description: LifeMinders is a service that delivers selected information to people who sign up. The service is free to subscribers. LifeMinders produces income via the advertising included in the free-information service.

Advertising that is attached to subject specific e-mail that consumers sign up for can be effective. Many advertisers get good results from specific e-mail advertising campaigns.

To find out more about this service, click the *Advertising/Sales* link at the bottom of the listed page.

MediaPost

Website: http://www.mediapost.com/

Keywords: Media and Advertising Information

Description: MediaPost is a leading advertising and media portal. It requires you to sign up for a free membership to access the information and resources on its website.

If you do a substantial amount of advertising, it will be worth registering at this site.

6.9 MEDIA SEARCH (NEWSPAPERS, MAGAZINES, ETC.)

Gebbie Press

Website: http://www.gebbieinc.com/

Keywords: Media Search Website

Description: The Gebbie Press website enables you to search for the websites of newspapers, TV stations, radio stations and magazines. The magazine search tool enables you to search for periodicals by subject. Select a subject to see a list of related periodicals. Click on a specific periodical to view its website.

Magazine and periodical websites are generally good sources of information. After finding these sites you may want to bookmark them or save them as favorites for easy access.

To find a media-related website, select the media type under Media Links at the bottom of the left navigation bar.

*Media Finder

Website: http://www.mediafinder.com/

Keywords: Media Locator (newspapers, magazines, newsletters, etc.)

Description: Media Finder is an excellent media locator service. To view the full listings, you'll have to subscribe to the service. If you don't subscribe, you'll have to locate the websites and contact information yourself.

Your local library is another option. Most libraries carry a print version of The Standard Periodical Directory, which is published by Oxbridge Communications, Inc.

SRDS

Website: http://www.srds.com

Keywords: Media Resource Guides

Description: SRDS offers a variety of media resource guides that will help you plan the placement of advertising in various publications. If you're placing a substantial amount of advertising, it may be worth purchasing one. SRDS's publications aren't cheap.

News Directory

Website: http://www.newsdirectory.com/

Keywords: Find Newspapers, Magazines and TV Stations

Description: The News Directory website enables you search for media sources. You can perform searches by title or area code. You can also search by selecting a subject or country.

6.10 WEB ADVERTISING INFORMATION

Adbility

Website: http://www.adbility.com/

Keywords: Web Advertising Information

Description: Adbility provides information and resources related to web advertising. Its website contains information on ad networks, affiliate programs, search engines, ad serving, banner ad creation, log analysis, site monitoring, instant content, counters and trackers.

Advertising Secrets

Website: http://advertisingsecrets.com/

Keywords: Advertising and Marketing-Related Articles

Description: The Advertising Secrets website has useful articles related to online advertising and marketing. The information on this site is useful, easy to find and easy to read.

*Avant/Marketer

Website: http://www.avantmarketer.com/

Keywords: Online Advertising Articles (excellent)

Description: Avant/Marketer has some impressive articles related to online advertising and related subjects. To access the search feature, scroll down on the listed page and click a *Read Full Article* link. Article pages feature text search boxes where you can type in a search subject.

The articles on this site are excellent. They're well-written and concise. Anyone considering an online advertising campaign should read some of the articles on this site.

CyberAtlas

Website: http://cyberatlas.internet.com/

Keywords: Web Advertising Articles

Description: If you're trying to come up with a web advertising strategy, don't forget to visit CyberAtlas.

Scroll down until you see the CyberAtlas navigation bar on the left. Click on the *Archives* link. The archives page contains links to pages with articles on advertising, demographics, geographics, hardware, traffic patterns, retailing, small business and more.

The articles on this site are good. There's a lot of useful information that will help you develop an online advertising strategy.

Internet Advertising Report

Website: http://www.internetnews.com/IAR/

Keywords: Internet Advertising Information/E-mail Newsletter

Description: The Internet Advertising Report is an information site that contains articles related to Internet advertising. You can also sign up to receive the company's e-mail newsletter.

Online Advertising Discussion List

Website: http://www.o-a.com/

Keywords: Online Advertising Discussion List

Description: If you're serious about online advertising, you might want to consider joining this list. It is a professional discussion of advertising strategies, results, studies, tools, and media coverage. It has over 7,500 participants.

6.11 WEB ADVERTISING SELECTION

TheAdStop.com

Website: http://www.theadstop.com/

Keywords: Advertising Service Selection

Description: TheAdStop.com gives you an overview/comparison of advertising services. Select an advertising category from the drop-down list in the upper left corner to see a list of related service providers.

Some of the advertising categories I reviewed listed some good options. Depending on what you're advertising, this site might list an ideal option.

This site also has a good resource page. Scroll down to the *Industry Info* section in the right navigation bar. Click on the *Resource Center* link to view its collection of advertising-related resources.

6.12 WEB ADVERTISING SERVICES

Ad Up

Website: http://www.ad-up.com/

Keywords: Web Advertising Service (full-service)

Description: Ad Up is a full-service web advertising service. Send the company a graphic and select your target audience, and it'll do the rest. Ad Up offers guaranteed results, advanced targeting, control over ad placement and timing, real-time reports, and the ability to make changes.

AdJuggler

Website: http://www.adjuggler.com/index.htm

Keywords: Web Advertising Service (geographic targeting capabilities)

Description: AdJuggler has a software application, hosted service, and global distribution network for web advertisers. This service enables advertisers to geographically target users around the world. It also offers advanced reporting capabilities.

AdJuggler's pricing plans are one aspect of its service that caught my attention. Its low-end option gives small site owners an affordable way to test the effectiveness of an online advertising campaign. Some of the ad services that were reviewed won't do anything for less than $2,000.

Commission Junction

Website: http://www.cj.com/index.asp

Keywords: Web Ad Tracking and Reporting

Description: Commission Junction offers a pay-for-performance service where marketers pay for results. Participating websites advertise a product or service offered by another website. In return, this service provider receives a commission for sales or leads. Commission Junction also offers a feature that enables you to view average earnings per 100 clicks for advertisers, publishers and individual ads.

If you're considering a substantial online promotion for a product or service offered at a website, this service is worth considering.

DoubleClick

Website: http://www.doubleclick.com/us/

Keywords: Banner Ad Serving and Measurement

Description: DoubleClick is an established service that provides banner ad serving and measurement tools. It provides tools and services to target, serve and analyze online advertising. You can choose from full-service and self-service options.

Fast Click

Website: http://www.fastclick.com/index.html

Keywords: Web Advertising Service

Description: Fast Click is a web-based application that implements, manages, optimizes and reports on web advertising campaigns. Members can change or create campaigns 24/7, remove or add banners, check campaign reports, etc.

24/7 Real Media

Website: http://www.247realmedia.com/

Keywords: Web Advertising Products and Services (high-end)

Description: 24/7 Real Media offers targeted campaigns to customers looking for high response, content alignment and quality brand affiliation. Its services and solutions are advanced solutions. The company also offers other services for online marketers.

6.13 WEB ADVERTISING SOLUTIONS/ PRODUCTS

AdRelevance

Website: http://www.adrelevance.com/

Keywords: Ad Intelligence Services (high-end)

Description: AdRelevance offers services to help web advertisers understand and monitor competitor ad campaigns, web traffic changes, etc. AdRelevance is an advanced service. If you want to know who, what, why, when and where in relation to an ad campaign, check out this firm's services. If you're planning to spend big money on web advertising, this service is worth considering.

International Business

7.1 ADVERTISING SLOGAN SEARCH

ADSlogans Unlimited

Website: http://www.adslogans.co.uk/index.html

Keywords: ADSlogans Search U.K.

Description: ADSlogans Unlimited is a service firm that specializes in ad slogan searches and strategies. If you plan to promote a product or service in the U.K., this might be a service worth considering. A company doing business in the U.S. might benefit from using these services also.

7.2 CONVERSION INFORMATION & TOOLS

Oanda

Website: http://www.oanda.com/

Keywords: Currency Conversion Tools and Information

Description: Oanda.com features a variety of tools and information related to currency conversion. The company offers a currency converter, currency cheat sheet, travel expense manager, currency data services, customizable tools, free converters and more.

Mega Converter 2

Website: http://www.megaconverter.com/Mega2/

Keywords: Conversion Tools and Information

Description: Mega Converter 2 has tools to convert currency, date, time, language, area, length, weight and more. If you're trying to sell a product to other countries, this site has useful features to help you with hundreds of conversions.

Time Zone Converter

Website: http://www.timezoneconverter.com/

Keywords: Time Zone Information and Tools

Description: The Time Zone Converter enables you to quickly find out what time it is in various time zones.

Tyzo

Website: http://www.tyzo.com/dir.html

Keywords: Travel and Conversion Information

Description: The Tyzo website features conversion information and tools. Areas covered include clothing sizes (international), a currency converter, dialing codes, electricity requirements, language, maps, metric conversion, time zones, weather, and world public holidays.

7.3 DEMOGRAPHIC INFORMATION (INTERNATIONAL)

International Data Base

Website: http://www.census.gov/ipc/www/idbnew.html

Keywords: International Demographic Information

Description: This site is a good place to start a search for demographic information on foreign countries. The *Product Catalog* link at the bottom of the page takes you to a catalog page where you can view the products offered by the U.S. Census Bureau.

If you can't find what you're looking for, click the *Contact Us* link to request more information.

7.4 FOREIGN COUNTRIES (INFORMATION)

*Country Studies

Website: http://lcweb2.loc.gov/frd/cs/cshome.html

Keywords: Country Information (global)

Description: The Library of Congress maintains The Country Studies website. It contains an extensive amount of information related to countries around the world.

The information provided is easy to find. This is one of the most complete and useful country information sites that I have seen.

Country Watch

Website: http://www.countrywatch.com/cw_default.asp

Keywords: Information on Foreign Countries

Description: Country Watch provides information about each of the 192 countries of the world. Select a country from the drop-down list at the top of the page to view the related information. This site is an excellent starting point if you need information on a country.

Country Watch charges to access the advanced features and services but it provides a lot of useful information without subscribing.

Embassy.org

Website: http://www.embassy.org/embassies/

Keywords: U.S. Embassy Finder

Description: Embassy.org is a good place to locate foreign embassies located in the U.S.

Euromonitor

Website: http://www.euromonitor.com/default.asp

Keywords: Country and Market Information

Description: Euromonitor provides country and market information. The free country profiles contain basic demographic, economic and limited market information. You can also search for reports related to countries and large markets. You'll have to pay for the listed reports.

Euromonitor is a provider of global strategic research. This company provides high-end research services and published information.

ExecutivePlanet.com

Website: http://www.executiveplanet.com/index2.jsp

Keywords: Cultural Information Site

Description: Do you need to know what to do or how to act when traveling or doing business abroad? If so, ExecutivePlanet.com is an excellent place to start. Its website provides you with cultural guidelines by country.

7.5 GLOBAL MARKETING

GlobalReach.com

Website: http://glreach.com/eng/ed/art.php3

Keywords: Articles on Global Marketing

Description: The listed page contains numerous articles on global marketing. If you have a concern or question related to selling abroad from a website, or attracting foreigners to a website, this is a good place to look. The articles reviewed were thorough, informative and well written.

7.6 GLOBAL PUBLICATIONS & PERIODICALS

Bowker's Global Books in Print

Website: http://www.globalbooksinprint.com/

Keywords: Book Search Site (global)

Description: The Bowker's Books in Print website is a good place to do an extensive search for available publications. It is a great place to find publications related to a foreign country or specific subject.

You'll have to sign up for a courtesy trial to use the features of this site.

Ulrich's Periodical Directory

Website: http://www.ulrichsweb.com/ulrichsweb/

Keywords: Global Periodical Search (global)

Description: The Ulrich's Periodical Directory website is a comprehensive source of information on serials (periodicals) throughout the world. If you're interested in doing business in a foreign country, this is a good place to find specialized information sources.

You'll have to sign up to use this site. The company offers a limited trial option that enables you to try these services for a limited period.

7.7 IMPORT/EXPORT (FINANCIAL SERVICES)

*Export-Import Bank of the United States

Website: http://65.170.103.143/index.html

Keywords: Import/Export Financial Services (official U.S. Bank)

Description: The Export-Import Bank provides guarantees of working capital loans for U.S. exporters. The organization guarantees the repayment of loans and makes loans to purchasers of U.S. goods and services. This organization also provides credit insurance that protects U.S. exporters against the risks of non-payment by foreign buyers.

The Export-Import Bank will finance the export of all types of non-military goods.

Two of the primary goals of Export-Import Bank are to:
1. Increase the export of environmental goods and services.
2. Expand the number of U.S. small businesses using its programs.

7.8 IMPORT/EXPORT (GENERAL)

BizEurope

Website: http://www.bizeurope.com/

Keywords: Import/Export Information and Services

Description: BizEurope offers an array of information and services for importers and exporters. Its membership fee is reasonable and the described services are substantial. Its website offers enough information without being a member that you can get a good idea of the benefits that members receive.

International Business Forum

Website: http://www.ibf.com/

Keywords: International Business Resources/Products and Service Postings

Description: The International Business Forum is a basic website but it contains listings that might create significant opportunity for the right person or company. It features listings for countries and organizations interested in buying and selling various products and services.

Turbolinker

Website: http://www.turbolinker.com/

Keywords: Import/Export Sites

Description: Turbolinker contains a massive amount of links to sites related to importing and exporting globally. The links, however, do not have text descriptions. You'll have to find what you're looking for by trial and error.

7.9 IMPORT/EXPORT INFORMATION

Bureau of Industry and Security (U.S. Department of Commerce)

Website: http://www.bxa.doc.gov

Keywords: Import/Export Information, Forms, Seminar Information, etc.

Description: This site contains an abundant amount of information related to importing and exporting products and services. You can download various forms necessary for exporting, contact regional offices to speak with an export counselor, sign up for seminars and more.

*BuyUSA

Website: http://www.buyusa.com/cgi-bin/db2www/index.d2w/input

Keywords: Listing and Support Services for Exporters

Description: Buy USA brings buyers and sellers together in a powerful online environment backed by the U.S. Department of Commerce. The organization offers U.S. suppliers and international companies free membership, which allows them to search for companies, create online contact lists and promote their company free of charge on BuyUSA.

Market Research: Click the *Market Research* link to see if the firm can help. The U.S. Commercial Services Flexible Market Research can provide you with answers about various markets free of charge.

This site also contains useful information and links.

Export.gov

Website: http://www.export.gov/index.html

Keywords: Export Information and Services (excellent site)

Description: The Small Business Administration operates Export.gov. Its website contains information and resources of interest to individuals and organizations interested in selling products or services in other countries. You can find information related to export counseling, export promotion programs and services, country and industry market research, finance and insurance trade agreements, trade statistics, trade events, export basics, foreign currency rates, international contacts, industry sector offices and contacts, tariffs and taxes, export documentation, U.S. export controls, schedule B (shipper's export declaration), NAFTA rules of origin, foreign trade advocacy, export assistance offices worldwide, etc.

Subscription Services: You can subscribe to the Export.gov newsletter and sign up for webcasts on exporting. You can also access the organization's archive of Export.gov newsletters.

ExportHotline

Website: http://www.exporthotline.com/index.html

Keywords: Country Reports and Statistics

Description: ExportHotline offers country reports, statistics, and related information. It requires you to register to use these services. If you can't find the information you need elsewhere, you might find it here.

Export Training Webcast

Website:
http://www.globalspeak.com/html/export-gov/ExportBasics.htm

Keywords: Export Information

Description: The Export Training Webcast is good way to get started on an export plan. Subjects covered: Taking the First Steps, How to Create an Export Strategy, Selling to Foreign Markets, Selling Services to the World, Getting Your Product Ready, Export Logistics, Types of Export Financing, Where and How to Obtain Export Financing, Export Insurance, Getting Paid, Working in a Foreign Culture, Documentation, Becoming an E-Exporter, Traveling Abroad, Negotiating the Deal, and Building Relationships

*ExportZone

Website: http://www.exportzone.com/

Keywords: Import/Export Information and Resources

Description: ExportZone offers information and resources for importers and exporters. The information and links are divided into two categories. Importing to the U.S. and exporting from the U.S.

Categories covered include; trade leads, product assistance, corporate assistance, USA regional assistance, federal assistance, international assistance, legal assistance, financial assistance, NAFTA assistance, currency assistance, forwarding assistance, upcoming tradeshows, travel assistance, how to, online publications, software, and quality links.

Import Administration

Website: http://ia.ita.doc.gov/

Keywords: Import Information and Related Data

Description: The Import Administration website contains information and data for importers, exporters, individuals, and organizations interested in doing business internationally. It provides links to government data on importing, administrative protective orders, antidumping, currency exchange rates, a document library, expected wages, federal register notices, glossary of terms and phrases, laws and regulations, statistics, USDOC person finder and more.

Import/Export Mailing List

Website: http://www.shipsolutions.com/messageboard.html

Keywords: Import/Export Information

Description: Looking for answers to your import/export questions or problems? The *Import-Export Mailing List* is a good place to start. After you register for the list, you can post questions and read the questions and answers posted by related professionals.

International Trade Data System

Website: http://www.itds.treas.gov/tradedata.html

Keywords: International Trade Publications

Description: The ITDS website enables you to order publications related to online trade and tariff data, metropolitan area exports, imports and exports by agricultural program and products, foreign trade statistics, imports and exports by mode of transportation, statistical programs, analytical reports and studies, trade data by textile and apparel quotas, tariff and non-tariff measures, import flows by origin for more than 100 countries, and a national trade estimate report on foreign trade barriers,

Regent Commerce Network

Website: http://www.china-inc.com/

Keywords: China Trade Information

Description: The Regent Commerce Network works to support business between North American and Chinese enterprises. The *Business Resources* link takes you to a page that lists link pages. The *Other Resources* link on the *Business Resources* page takes you to a page with numerous useful links.

This site also has useful information about China and trade shows.

Hong Kong Trade Development Council

Website: http://www.tdctrade.com/index.htm

Keywords: Hong Kong Trade Information and Opportunities

Description: This site contains a tremendous amount of information related to international trade with Hong Kong. The links under the *TDC Cyber Marketplace* sub-heading give you a good idea of the trade opportunities available.

TradePort

Website: http://www.tradeport.org/ts/index.html

Keywords: Export Information, Market Research, Trade Leads

Description: Trade Port contains information and links of interest to individuals and companies exporting a product or service. If you're not using Netscape Navigator, you might want to scroll to the bottom of the page and view the text edition of the site.

Its website features links to trade events, world news, references, company searches, a bookstore, job opportunities, mailing lists and export assistance.

U.S. Business Advisor

Website: http://www.business.gov/busadv/index.cfm

Keywords: Business Assistance, International Trade

Description: The U.S. Business Advisor website contains information and resources related to business development, financial assistance, laws and regulations, international trade, buying and selling, agencies and gateways, e-services, learning the Internet and more.

Click on the *Agencies and Gateways* link to view a scrolling list of government agencies and information sources.

The e-services link takes you to a page of articles, links and information related to doing business online.

7.10 Import/Export (services & portals)

AsianNet Trade InfoCenter

Website: http://www.asiannet.com/infocenter/

Keywords: Product Searches (buy and sell), Trade Resources

Description: AsianNet contains useful resources related to International Trade. Click the *Want to Buy* tab at the top of the page to search for products by category. You can post offers to sell, free of charge.

The *Trade Info Tools* link in the left navigation bar takes you to a page with useful links. It contains categories related to currency conversion, exchange rates, trade shows, time zones, international country codes and international ports. Click on a category to view a list of links.

EcKorea

Website: http://www.eckorea.net/

Keywords: Korea Import/Export Information and Resources

Description: ecKorea operates a marketplace where you can post offers and search for products being offered. Click on the *Marketplace* tab to view the marketplace page. Its website also features information about Korea.

With a free membership you can build a free home page, make electronic catalogs, store offers, directories, and catalogs, and use the EC Plaza e-mail service. Paid membership extends these benefits and adds others.

Global Sources

Website: http://www.globalsources.com/

Keywords: Product Locator (China, global)

Description: Global Sources is a good place to look for products to import. If you're interested in making volume purchases to resell, this site is a good place to look. You'll find computer products, electronic components, electronics, fashion accessories and supplies, timepieces, gifts, home products, and hardware-related items.

Many of products listed on this site are manufactured in China. You can search for products manufactured in 185 countries.

Import/Export Bulletin Board

Website: http://trade.swissinfo.net/

Keywords: Buy and Sell Listings, Business Opportunities

Description: This is a great site for individuals or businesses interested in buying or selling products globally. The *Offers to Buy* section lists individuals and businesses interested in purchasing products and services. The *Offers to Sell* section lists individuals and businesses interested in selling products and services. The *Business Opportunities* section lists various business opportunities.

Planet Business

Website: http://www.planetbiz.com/index.html

Keywords: Import/Export Product Listings

Description: Planet Business (PB) lists a variety of products in various categories. PB is a product listing site and marketplace for importers, exporters, traders and distributors. Its website lists hundreds of products that are available, but they're not specifically categorized.

Taiwan Commerce

Website: http://www.commerce.com.tw/

Keywords: Import/Export Portal (Taiwan)

Description: Taiwan Commerce provides business information and services for companies interested in doing business with Taiwan. The site contains buy/sell and business opportunity listings. It also lists business services. You can search for products you'd like to import and list products you would like to export.

If you're interested in doing business with Taiwan, this is a great place to start. The membership fees are reasonable, and the company offers an array of useful information and services.

Thomas Global Register

Website: http://www.aernet.com/

Keywords: Manufacturer and Distributor Directory

Description: The Thomas Global Register is a directory of 500,000 manufacturers and distributors from 26 countries. It is an excellent resource for buyers and sellers of industrial products.

Trade Sources

Website: http://www.tradesources.com/default.asp

Keywords: Product Searches and Related Resources

Description: Trade Sources is a good place to search for product suppliers in Honk Kong, Mainland China and Taiwan. Its website also offers trade advice, translation services, information, and related resources. You'll have to register to use all of the features offered at this site.

If you're interested in importing or exporting to Hong Kong, China, or Taiwan, this site has a lot to offer.

7.11 IMPORT/EXPORT (TOOLS & SERVICES)

Alibaba.com

Website: http://www.alibaba.com

Keywords: Export Supplier Portal (information and resource site)

Description: Alibaba.com is a marketplace for global trade and a provider of online marketing services for importers and exporters. Its website lists an extensive amount of products and services of interest to importers and exporters.

eTraderoom

Website: http://www.etraderoom.com/index.html

Keywords: Import/Export Collaboration Tool

Description: eTraderoom is a web-based solution for global trade management. It is a hosted service that provides users with a workflow management system that self-directs the importer or exporter through the trade process. It's affordable and designed for large and small businesses that are looking to export a product or service. eTraderoom is an easy to use, cost-efficient way to turn international inquiries into sales.

7.12 INTERNATIONAL BUSINESS INFORMATION

Everything International

Website: http://faculty.philau.edu/russowl/russow.html

Keywords: International Business Information

Description: Everything International is an international business resource website. It contains hundreds of links to sites and pages with useful information. If you can't find what you're looking for anywhere else, you might be able to find it here.

*Federation of International Trade Associations (FITA)

Website: http://www.fita.org/index.html

Keywords: Trade Associations, Market Research Resources, etc.

Description: FITA has a great website. It has an index of 4,000 web resources, international market research resources, articles about international trade, a directory of international trade associations in North America, directory of export management companies and more.

The fita.org website is well-organized and easy to use. It contains a vast amount of useful information for anyone doing business globally.

*International Affairs Resources

Website: http://www.etown.edu/vl/

Keywords: International Affairs and Relations

Description: The IAR website contains links to websites related to international affairs. This site is an excellent place to start a search for country specific information. Short and effective descriptions are provided for most of the listed links.

*International Trade Centre

Website: http://www.intracen.org/

Keywords: International Trade and Business Information

Description: The World Trade Organization (WTO) and the United Nations (UN) operate the International Trade Centre. The ITC website contains information related to product and market development, development of trade support services, trade information, human resource development, international purchasing and supply management, needs assessment, and program design for trade promotion.

The ITC offers an abundant amount of quality information and resources for anyone wanting to do business internationally.

Wisconsin Department of Commerce

Website: http://www.commerce.state.wi.us/ie/ie-org.html

Keywords: International Trade Information

Description: The Wisconsin Department of Commerce website has hundreds of links to websites related to international business. It lists links related to expanding export sales, overseas markets, export data, trade shows and events, newsletters, international business links, trade leads, trade financing and more.

7.13 INTERNATIONAL COMPANY & PRODUCT INFORMATION

Kompass

Website: http://www.kompass.com/kinl/

Keywords: Company and Product Information

Description: The Kompass website contains a wealth of information related to companies and various types of products. You can search for companies around the world that sell or manufacture products in various countries and more.

7.14 INTERNATIONAL ECONOMICS

Deardorff's Glossary of International Economics

Website: http://www-personal.umich.edu/~alandear/glossary/

Keywords: International Economics Terminology and Definitions

Description: The listed website provides definitions for words and terms related to international economics.

7.15 INTERNATIONAL TRADEMARKS

TradeName.com

Website: http://www.tradename.com/

Keywords: International Trademark Information and Resources

Description: Tradename.com is an e-commerce intellectual property service. This company provides worldwide trademark-related services. The services offered include searches, registrations, assignments, and management services. Its website contains useful links, a questions and answers section, and other useful information.

7.16 International Trade Leads (buyers & sellers)

Worldbid.com

Website: http://www.worldbid.com/

Keywords: International Sales Leads, Buyers and Sellers

Description: Worldbid.com posts products and services that are for sale and wanted by organizations around the world. It is a fee service but the price is reasonable if you're seeking, or providing, products or services of substantial value.

7.17 Market Research Service Locator

World Opinion

Website: http://www.worldopinion.com/

Keywords: Market Research Resources (global), E-research Tools

Description: This is a good place to locate market research companies around the world. The *Directory* tab will take you to a page where you can search for market research companies worldwide.

7.18 Shipping

See Shipping (Business Information Section)

7.19 TRADE BARRIERS, TARIFFS AND RESTRICTIONS

*Market Access Sectoral and Trade Barriers Database

Website: http://mkaccdb.eu.int/mkdb/mkdb.pl

Keywords: Country Specific Market Information

Description: The Market Access Sectoral and Trade Barriers Database gives you access to market information by country. Its website provides information related to trade barriers, restrictions, quotas, tariffs and related issues.

This is a great place to get an overview of the laws and restrictions involved with selling to a specific country.

7.20 TRADE PROFESSIONALS/TRADE COMPANY RECRUITING

Fortuna

Website: http://fortuna.frinet.org/

Keywords: Trade Professionals and Trade Company Recruiting Information

Description: Are you a trade professional looking for opportunity or a trade company looking for the right trade professional? If so, Fortuna might be able to help. Fortuna is a service that brings trade professionals and trade companies together. It is a fee service.

7.21 TRADE SHOW INFORMATION

*Trade Show News Network (TSNN)

Website: http://www2.tsnn.com/

Keywords: Trade Show-Related Information and Resources

Description: The TSNN website enables you to search for trade shows and related suppliers. You can also list and search for products and services in various categories. Its website gives you access to resources, publications, related associations, international trade show information and more.

There is a vast amount of information, resources and services featured on this site. It offers information, features and services that most businesses could benefit from. If you're interested in marketing products or services to national or international markets, this site has a lot to offer.

7.22 TRANSLATION SERVICES

Babel Fish Translation Tools

Website: http://babel.altavista.com/tr

Keywords: Translation Tools and Software

Description: Need to translate a block of text or a web page? The Babel Fish website features an easy to use tool that you can use to translate a message from English to other languages or vice-versa.

Inter Tran

Website: http://www.tranexp.com:2000/intertran

Keywords: Translation Tools, Software and Portable Hardware

Description: The Inter Tran website has a feature that will translate a block of text or an entire web page. It also offers a variety of software and portable translation devices.

Live Interpreter Now

Website: http://www.livelanguagenow.com/main.html

Keywords: Professional Language Interpreters (fee service)

Description: Live Interpreter Now has professional interpreters for more than 140 languages. To use this service you call Live Interpreter, establish credit information and tell the service provider what you're trying to accomplish. You're then provided with a translator that will place a call or listen in on a conversation via speakerphone or dual handset.

ProZ

Website: http://www.proz.com/

Keywords: Site for Language Professionals

Description: The *Ask Kudoz* features of this site enable you to get the cultural or unspoken meaning of a term or phrase in a language. For instance, a foreigner might ask, what do Americans mean by a *fork in the road* when they're talking about their life?

ProZ is a good place to go if you're looking for a language professional to fill a position. It's also a good place to find a job if you're a language professional.

7.23 U.K. MARKETING, ADVERTISING, AND MEDIA

Brand Republic

Website: http://www.brandrepublic.com/home/index.cfm

Keywords: Marketing, Advertising and Media Information

Description: The Brand Republic website is a U.K. marketing, advertising, and media information site that is updated daily. The library section allows subscribers to search the archive of Campaign, Marketing, PR Week, and Revolution magazines. To access it, click *Search News Archive* from the *News* drop-down list.

The related U.K. periodicals published by Haymark Publishing are listed in the periodicals section. You can check out its other publications at http://www.brandrepublic.com/shop/.

Institute of Sales Promotion (ISP)

Website: http://www.isp.org.uk/

Keywords: U.K. Sales Promotions

Description: The ISP website features a links page that lists a variety of organizations of interest to individuals or companies promoting products or services in the U.K.

The ISP is an organization for individuals and companies involved with promotions in the U.K. It promotes responsible practices and provides members with legal advice services.

Marketing Yellow Pages

Section 8

Promotional Materials

8.1 Communications Materials

ImageX

Website: http://www.imagex.com/

Keywords: Production and Distribution of Communications Materials

Description: ImageX provides web-based services to help you manage the production and distribution of communications materials.

The ImageX Marketing System enables organizations to segment their sales organization for targeted distribution of printed and digital information, improve communication with sales partners, and track the cost and usage of materials by the sales force.

The ImageX Print System enables companies to order, manage and distribute branded communications materials such as stationary and business cards. It also offers print services to provide efficient, cost-effective print production and delivery.

8.2 COPYWRITING SERVICES (SALES & MARKETING)

AdCopyWriting.com

Website: http://www.adcopywriting.com/

Keywords: Copywriting Tips, Services, Consulting (U.K.)

Description: AdCopyWriting.com provides useful information and tips to help you write effective sales copy. The *Articles* link takes you to a page that lists useful articles related to copywriting.

This company also provides copywriting and consulting services.

Creative Marketing Solutions

Website: http://www.yudkin.com/marketing.htm

Keywords: Naming, Sales Letters, Publicity, and Logo Creation Tips

Description: The listed website provides practical advice to help you name a product, service, or business. It's a good place to start if you need ideas.

Creative Marketing Solutions also provides a variety of marketing-related services. The services offered include professional input on marketing materials, marketing strategies, and websites.

You'll also find marketing-related books, articles, and audiotapes.

Drum Creative Communications

Website: http://www.drum-corp.net/

Keywords: Creative Strategies, Slogans, Advertising, Direct Mail, etc.

Description: If you're planning a marketing strategy for a medium-to-large business, Drum Creative Communications is worth considering. This firm's client list and work samples clearly indicate that the company is capable of handling medium-to-large-sized creative projects.

If you have a substantial project and an appropriate budget, these services are worth considering.

Sig Rosenblum

Website: http://www.sigrosenblum.com/

Keywords: Direct Sales and Marketing Copy

Description: Sig Rosenblum offers copywriting services. If you're looking for someone to write copy for a sales letter, brochure, or promotional piece, his services are worth considering. I reviewed some of his work. It's apparent that he has a substantial amount of experience.

*Joe *Mr. Fire* Vitale

Website: http://www.mrfire.com/index.html

Keywords: Copywriting Information, Tips, Newsletters, Articles, etc.

Description: This site is an excellent place to find copywriting information and resources. It contains numerous articles to help you write effective sales copy. It also offers copywriting and marketing-related books, audiotapes, videos, e-books, etc.

This is a great resource for anyone trying to write sales copy. If you don't want to do it yourself, you might be able to get Mr. Fire to do it for you.

8.3 DESIGN & COPY PROFESSIONALS (RECRUITING)

Elance

Website: http://www.elance.com/

Keywords: Locate Professional Copywriters, Graphic Artists, Web professionals, etc.

Description: To locate a service provider, visit the Elance website and type in the service you're looking for in the marketplace search box. Elance connects buyers and service providers in hundreds of categories. Enter a job description and you'll receive bids from qualified service providers.

Kasamba

Website: http://www.kasamba.com/default.asp

Keywords: Locate Graphic Designers, Website Designers, Copywriters, etc.

Description: Kasamba is a good place to search for professionals to help you design graphics, logos, write sales copy, edit copy, etc. Its website enables you to search for professionals necessary to create brochures, logos, sales letters and more.

Portfolio.com

Website: http://www.portfolios.com/

Keywords: Locate Design and Copy Professionals

Description: Portfolio.com is a great place to find a design or copy professional. You can search for graphic designers, copywriters, photographers, industrial designers, illustrators, animators and more.

This service is free to users. The registered service providers pay for listings.

Writing Assistance Inc.

Website: http://www.writingassist.com/index.htm

Keywords: Contract and Permanent Communications Professionals

Description: Writing Assistance Inc. is an employment agency for communications professionals. The firm will help you find technical writers, marketing communications writers, training developers, project managers, website designers, content developers and graphic designers.

8.4 DESKTOP PUBLISHING

Desktop Publishing

Website: http://desktoppub.miningco.com/

Keywords: Desktop Publishing-Related Information

Description: The listed website contains an abundant amount of information and resources for desktop publishers and related professionals. The site covers software, design tips, production and more.

8.5 DOCUMENT TEMPLATES

Template Gallery

Website: http://officeupdate.microsoft.com/templategallery/

Keywords: Document Templates (Microsoft software)

Description: The Template Gallery has a variety of templates that you can download and use. The company offers templates for stationery, labels, cards, business forms, marketing materials, publications, education, legal forms, letters, planning documents, management documents, finance, accounting, resumes, cover letters, personal interests and more.

8.6 GRAPHIC DESIGN

Graphic Design (about.com)

Website: http://graphicdesign.about.com/

Keywords: Graphic Design Tips and Resources

Description: About.com's Graphic Design website features information and tips related to graphic design. There is and extensive amount of useful information on this site related to graphic design.

8.7 LOGO CREATION

Logo Works

Website: http://www.logoworks.com/

Keywords: Logo Design Services

Description: Logo Works is a logo design service. You can view samples of Logo Works' work on its website. The company offers timely service and a variety of pricing plans.

8.8 LOGO MERCHANDISE (PROMOTIONAL PRODUCTS)

GoPromos.com

Website: http://www.gopromos.com/

Keywords: Logo Merchandise/Promotional Products

Description: GoPromos offers a variety of printed promotional products. Its website features an extensive assortment of products that can be imprinted with your logo.

iPrint

Website: http://www102.iprint.com

Keywords: Logo Merchandise, Banners, Signs, etc.

Description: iPrint offers a variety of logo merchandise including banners and signs. Its prices for banners and signs are reasonable. If you're looking for a way to get your customers attention, this is a good place to look.

8.9 NEWSLETTER WRITING SERVICES

Put it in Writing

Website: http://www.put-it-in-writing.com/

Keywords: Newsletter Writing Service

Description: Put it in Writing is a full-service newsletter writing service. This company handles all aspects of production and printing. Newsletters can be an excellent way to promote your products or services.

8.10 PHOTOGRAPHIC IMAGES

Corbis

Website: http://pro.corbis.com/default.asp

Keywords: Photographic Images (single and CDs)

Description: Corbis.com features some impressive photographs and collections on CD that can be used for promotional materials. You will, however, have to sign up to view multiple photos in a selected category. Some of Corbis.com's photographs are royalty-free, while others involve rights and permissions.

*iStock

Website: http://www.istockphoto.com/

Keywords: Photographic Images You Can Download

Description: If you need a photographic image for your website or promotional materials, iStock is an excellent place to look. When you sign up, you will receive two download credits. After your credits are used, each additional download will cost you 50 cents. There are thousands of photos on this site. You can search by category to find a photo that suits your specific needs.

iStock lets you view a substantial amount of images without having to register. In addition, its policy for using images is favorable.

8.11 PHOTOGRAPHIC IMAGES & CLIPART

Design Gallery Live

Website: http://dgl.microsoft.com/

Keywords: Photographic Images and Clipart

Description: Design Gallery Live enables you to search for photographic images and clipart. The firm also has sounds and motions that can be used on websites. I could not find a pricing page or related information. My best guess is that you can download and use the items free of charge.

You may also want to check out its *Template Gallery*. You can access it from the navigation column on the left side of the page. It contains templates for operations forms, brochures, various promotional materials and more.

Press Releases

See Public Relations/Press Releases (marketing information section)

8.12 PRINTING (HIGH VOLUME)

Output Links

Website: http://www.outputlinks.com/

Keywords: High-Volume Printing Resources

Description: If you're looking for information and resources related to high-volume printing, Output Links is a good place to start. Its website is one of the most useful high-volume printing resources I've found.

Printing Information: If you point to the *Knowledge* link on the top navigation bar, you'll see drop-down list with a *Publications* link. Click on the *Publications* link to view multiple sources of printing information.

Service Providers: Point to the *Services* link on the top navigation bar to see a drop-down list. The drop-down list contains an *Outsourcing and Service Bureaus* link. Click on it to see a list of multiple service providers.

The high-volume computer output (HVOC) industry is the focus of this site, which is a resource for individuals and companies that buy, sell, use, and manage HVOC-related products and services. It is also of interest to individuals and businesses that provide HVOC-related consultation services.

HVOC documents are generally bills, statements, invoices, forms, financial documents, technical documents and other documents used to conduct business. Such documents generally have a short life and need to be regenerated periodically. Many types of promotional documents would fit into this category.

This site was listed because the websites of high-volume printers are confusing. It's hard to understand the products and services offered if you're unfamiliar with the industry. This site does a good job of bridging that gap.

8.13 Printing (promotional materials)

58K

Website: http://www.58k.com/

Keywords: Printing Bid Service

Description: 58K is a service that enables you to get bids on substantial print jobs. You can post your print job on 58K and get bids from printing services. This service is appropriate for most types of print jobs. The company doesn't encourage using this service for small jobs like personal stationary or highly sensitive jobs like design drawings.

If you're getting the run around or think your paying too much for local printing services, a service like the one offered by 58k might be the answer.

8.14 Printing (signs & lettering)

Kinkos

Website: http://www.kinkos.com/

Keywords: Printing Services, Signs, Lettering, etc.

Description: The Kinkos website enables you to order a variety of printed products online. The company offers printed materials, signs and lettering.

8.15 Visual Content

Thought Equity

Website: http://www.thoughtequity.com/index.html

Keywords: Visual Content for Promotional Materials, etc.

Description: Thought Equity offers ready-to-use visual content for promotional materials. You'll have to sign up to view its inventory.

Thought Equity's *Advertising Library* includes visual products for direct mail, e-mail marketing, newspaper, Internet, magazine, radio and TV.

Its *Marketing Library* includes business/product names and logos (including matching trademarks and domain names), products for websites, stationary packages, business packages, forms and agreements, and more.

Government Information

9.1 BUSINESS INFORMATION AND SERVICES

*Service Corps of Retired Executives (SCORE)

Website: http://www.score.org/

Keywords: Business Advice and Counseling

Description: SCORE is a program sponsored by the U.S. Small Business Administration to assist small businesses. Score has 10,500 volunteer business counselors that provide small business mentoring and advice. You can get advice via e-mail or in person.

Federal Trade Commission (FTC)

Website: http://www.ftc.gov/ftc/business.htm

Keywords: Advertising and Business Information

Description: The *Business Publications* link takes you to a page with a subject list. Click on a subject to view related titles. There is a lot of useful information related to advertising, doing business online and other subjects. You will also find information to help you avoid problems associated with improper advertising and marketing techniques.

Small Business Administration (SBA)

Website: http://www.sba.gov/library/pubs.html

Keywords: Business Information and Services

Description: The SBA offers a variety of business and marketing information. The SBA's publications page lists a variety of information related to business and marketing.

If you're a small business owner on a limited budget, don't forget to check out the various services that the SBA offers. The organization offers a variety of services for small business owners.

U.S. Business Advisor

Website: http://www.business.gov/busadv/index.cfm

Keywords: Business Assistance, International Trade

Description: The U.S. Business Advisor website contains information and resources related to business development, financial assistance, laws and regulations, international trade, buying and selling, agencies and gateways, e-services, learning the Internet and more.

Click on the *Agencies and Gateways* link to view a scrolling list of government agencies and information sources.

The e-services link takes you to a page of articles, links and information related to doing business online.

9.2 CENSUS INFORMATION

U.S. Census Bureau (demographic Information)

Website: http://www.census.gov/index.html

Keywords: Information and Reference Publications

Description: This site enables you to access TIGER (Topologically Integrated Geographic Encoding and Referencing System). The TIGER/Line files are a digital database of geographic features, such as roads, railroads, rivers, lakes, political boundaries, census statistical boundaries, etc. covering the entire United States. The U.S. Census Bureau website catalogs numerous reference publications. Many of the publications listed were not easy to find on other sites.

NAICS (North American Industry Classification System) The system that has replaced the U.S. Standard Industrial Classification (SIC) system.

E-Stats Research Papers: Measuring Electronic Business, etc.

The U.S. Census Bureau offers sector specific reports related to: Mining, utilities, construction, manufacturing, wholesale trade, retail trade, transportation and warehousing, information, finance and insurance, real estate, rentals and leasing, professional, scientific, technical services, management of companies and enterprises, administrative support, waste management, remediation services, educational services, health care, social assistance, arts, entertainment and recreation, accommodation and food services, other services (except public administration), and auxiliaries not in sector 55.

An entire section of this site enables you to download specific reports for specific areas.

9.3 DEMOGRAPHIC INFORMATION (INTERNATIONAL)

International Data Base

Website: http://www.census.gov/ipc/www/idbnew.html

Keywords: International Demographic Information

Description: The International Data Base is a good place to start your search for demographic information on foreign countries. The *Product Catalog* link at the bottom of the page takes you to the catalog page where you can view products offered by the U.S. Census Bureau.

If you can't find what you're looking for, click the *Contact Us* link to request more information.

9.4 IMPORT/EXPORT

Bureau of Industry and Security (U.S. Department of Commerce)

Website: http://www.bxa.doc.gov

Keywords: Import/Export Information, Forms, Seminars, etc.

Description: This site contains a wealth of information related to importing and exporting products. You can download various forms necessary for exporting, contact regional offices to speak with an export counselor, sign up for seminars, etc.

BuyUSA

Website: http://www.buyusa.com/

Keywords: U.S. and International Market Research Reports

Description: The U.S. Department of Commerce operates The BuyUSA website. The site contains information related to exporting and U.S. and International market research. You'll have to register to access the international market research section.

*Country Studies

Website: http://lcweb2.loc.gov/frd/cs/cshome.html

Keywords: Country Information (global)

Description: The Library of Congress maintains The Country Studies website. It contains an extensive amount of information related to countries around the world.

The information provided is easy to find. This is one of the most complete and useful country information sites that I have seen.

Embassy.org

Website: http://www.embassy.org/embassies/

Keywords: U.S. Embassy Finder

Description: This site enables you to locate foreign embassies located in the U.S.

Export.gov

Website: http://www.export.gov/index.html

Keywords: Export Information and Services (excellent site)

Description: The Small Business Administration operates Export.gov. It is an excellent resource for individuals or organizations interested in selling products or services in other countries. Export.gov provides information on export counseling, export promotion programs and services, country and industry market research, financing and insuring trade agreements, trade statistics, trade events, export basics, foreign currency rates, international contacts list, industry sector offices and contacts, tariffs and taxes, export documentation, U.S. export controls, schedule B (shipper's export declaration), NAFTA rules of origin, foreign trade advocacy, export assistance offices worldwide, etc.

Subscription Services: You can subscribe to the Export.gov newsletter and sign up for webcasts on exporting. You can also access archives of Export.gov newsletters.

Import Administration

Website: http://ia.ita.doc.gov/

Keywords: Import Information and Related Data

Description: This site contains an abundance of useful data for importers, exporters, individuals, and organizations interested in doing business internationally. It provides links to government data on importing, administrative protective orders, antidumping, currency exchange rates, a document library, expected wages, federal register notices, glossary of terms and phrases, laws and regulations, statistics, USDOC person finder and more.

United States Department of Commerce (USDOC)

Import/Export Trade Resources (U.S. Government)

Website: http://www.itds.treas.gov/itdssitemap.html

Keywords: Links to Import/Export-Related Sites

Description: This page contains links to useful sites related to importing and exporting. You can access information related to trade data, import resources, export resources, miscellaneous resources, country profiles, industry profiles and general import/export information.

International Trade Data System (ITDS)

Website: http://www.itds.treas.gov/tradedata.html

Keywords: International Trade Publications

Description: The ITDS website enables you to order publications related to online trade and tariff data, metropolitan area exports, imports and exports by agricultural program and products, foreign trade statistics, imports and exports by mode of transportation, statistical programs and analytical reports and studies, trade data by textile and apparel quotas, tariff and non-tariff measures, import flows by origin for more than 100 countries and a national trade estimate report on foreign trade barriers.

**National Technical Information Service (NTIS)

Website: http://www.ntis.gov/

Keywords: Government Publications (search for over 750,000 publications).

Description: After searching around this site a while, I found some valuable information related to specific markets and industries.

Publications like the *U.S. Industry and Trade Outlook* and the *Statistical Abstract of the United States* can be found and ordered from this site. Many publications can be downloaded directly from the site. I used the search mechanism for a while and wasn't real impressed. It is, however, sufficient to find common government publications.

Sample Search Results: I entered *marketing and computers* in the NTIS advanced search feature and 7702 results were found. After the first page, the listed results were very relevant. I found reports on computer-related exports to numerous countries, etc.

*U.S. Commercial Service

Website: http://www.usatrade.gov/

Keywords: Export Assistance, Consulting and Advocacy Services

Description: This is a good place to find out about government information and services related to exporting. Similar sites are listed but this one is well organized. If you're getting lost on the other .gov sites trying to find out about export assistance and programs, you might try this one.

9.5 SELLING TO THE GOVERNMENT

Federal Biz Opportunities

Website: http://www.fedbizopps.gov/

Keywords: Government Purchasing Site

Description: FedBizOpps.gov is a point-of-entry for Federal Government procurement opportunities. This site allows vendors to search, monitor and retrieve opportunities solicited by the federal government. Its Vendor Notification service will notify you about opportunities that match the criteria you select.

Finding a federal agency that is looking for a specific type of product or service might take a while. The functional features for vendors are a disappointing.

9.6 STATISTICAL INFORMATION

Bureau of Economic Analysis (BEA)

Website: http://www.bea.doc.gov/

Keywords: Statistical Information Products (diskettes, CD's, reports)

Description: If you're looking for statistical information about the U.S. economy, the BEA website is a good place to start. Reports include: Survey of Current Business, National Income and Product Accounts of the United States, Fixed Reproducible Tangible Wealth in the United States, Benchmark Input-Output Accounts of the United States, Foreign Direct Investment in the United States,

U.S. Direct Investment Abroad, *Gross Domestic Product by Industry*, State Personal Income, U.S. International Trade in Goods and Services, Real Inventories, Sales, Inventory-Sales Ratios for Manufacturing and Trade, and more.

Direct Mail

10.1 DIRECT MAIL INFORMATION

American List Counsel (ALC)

Website: http://www.amlist.com/

Keywords: Direct Mail and List Information

Description: The ALC Knowledge Center provides information related to data research, analysis, marketing and more. The company offers newsletters and reports, industry FAQs, a direct mail library, glossary of terms and an ask-an-expert service.

Direct Mail Data Solutions (DMDS)

Website: http://www.directmaildata.com/

Keywords: Direct Mail Information, Glossary, List Services

Description: The Direct Mail Data Solutions (DMDS) website features a *Direct Mail Fundamentals* and *Glossary* section. The direct mail fundamentals page features information related to the advantages of direct mail, DM target marketing, creative tips, increasing response, response rates, postal regulations and choosing a direct mail printer. The glossary page will help you understand related terminology.

*The Drayton Bird Partnership

Website: http://www.draytonbird.com/

Keywords: Direct Marketing Information

Description: This site contains excellent information related to marketing, direct marketing and direct mail. You'll have to click on one of the birds (top center) to enter the site. After you enter the site, click on the *277 Answers* link on the bottom of the page or the *Search* link.

Idea Site for Business

Website: http://www.ideasiteforbusiness.com/ideamenu.htm

Keywords: Direct Mail Tips

Description: The Idea Site for Business provides information and tips related to sales copy, direct mail, brochure design, writing and more. It also contains tips and articles related several aspects of marketing.

*Think Direct Marketing, Inc.

Website: http://www.thinkdirectmarketing.com/index.shtml

Keywords: Direct Mail Information

Description: The DM Library link on the listed page takes you to a page where you can find information related to privacy, direct marketing practices, industry reports, case studies and more. It also offers DM tutorials, a recommended reading section, postal information, a resource section and interactive tools.

10.2 DIRECT MAIL PLANNING

Business Mail 101

Website: http://www.usps.com/

Keywords: Direct Mail Planning Tips

Description: The USPS website provides information to help businesses plan direct mail packages and campaigns. Select *All Products and Services* on the top navigation bar to see an overview of its information and services. On the *All Products and Services* page select *Business Tools*.

10.3 DIRECT MAIL QUOTES

*DirectMailQuotes.com

Website: http://www.directmailquotes.com/

Keywords: Direct Mail Project Bid Service

Description: DirectMailQuotes.com is a service that enables you to get quotes from multiple service providers. A party interested in a quote chooses specifications that are sent out to multiple service providers that bid on the project.

Think Direct Marketing, Inc.

Website: http://www.thinkdirectmarketing.com/index.shtml

Keywords: Direct Mail Project Quotes, Related Information, NCOA Services

Description: Think Direct Marketing offers a direct marketing quote service where you can get multiple bids on a direct mail project. It also offers mailing lists, related services and information related to direct mailing.

National Change of Address (NCOA)

10.4 DIRECT MAIL SERVICE (FULL-SERVICE)

Zairmail

Website: http://biz.zairmail.com/

Keywords: Direct Mail Service (design and send)

Description: Zairmail enables you to design and send a direct mail package from your desktop. You can select criteria for a custom mailing list or have the mailing sent to an existing customer list. This service is convenient and reasonably priced.

If you choose to use a print and send service, remember to put some time and effort into the materials you're sending.

10.5 MAIL ORDER TERMINOLOGY

Mail Order Dictionary

Website: http://www.howtoadvice.com/MailOrderDictionary

Keywords: Mail Order Terminology

Description: Wondering what a mail order-related term or phrase means? The Mail Order Dictionary defines basic words and terms commonly associated with mail order.

10.6 POSTAL INFORMATION

United States Postal Service

Website: http://www.usps.com/

Keywords: Postal and Business Information

Description: The USPS website is a good place to look for information related to mailing, address information and management, mail preparation, and more.

United States Postal Service Direct Mail site

Website: http://www.usps.com/directmail/

Keywords: Direct Mail Information and Resources

Description: The USPS direct mail website offers an array of resources for businesses interested in direct mail. Its website features a direct mail guide, DM templates, DM FAQs, DM resources, DM glossary, DM seminars, DM merchants, rates, mailing information and more.

Zip Code Finder

Website: http://www.usps.com/ncsc/lookups/lookup_ctystzip.html

Keywords: City/State Zip Code Finder

Description: Need to find a zip code. This site has a feature that enables you to search for zip codes by city and state.

10.7 POST CARDS

*Modern Post Card

Website: http://www.modernpostcard.com/

Keywords: Postcard Printing and Mailing Service

Description: Modern Post Card offers quality postcard printing and mailing services. Its website features information to help you plan an effective postcard marketing strategy. You can design you own postcards or have Modern Post Card do it.

Think Direct Mail, Inc.

Website: http://www.thinkdirectmail.com/oms/

Keywords: Direct Mail Design Tools (design and send)

Description: Think Direct Mail, Inc. offers tools and services to help you design, print, and mail postcards right from your desktop. The firm also has a template library for creating postcards, newsletters, self-mailers and more. Using the services requires you to register and have a list of where the items will be sent.

Web Marketing Strategy

11.1 AFFILIATE PROGRAMS

Wilson Web

Website: http://www.wilsonweb.com/

Keywords: Affiliate Programs/Web Marketing Information

Description: Wilson Web offers useful information to help you promote a website. It also offers information related to affiliate programs, web marketing, e-commerce and more. Much of the information contained on the site is for members only.

The affiliate management resources listed in the right column toward the bottom of the page will give you insight on starting an affiliate program.

Associate Programs

Website: http://www.associateprograms.com/index.shtml

Keywords: Affiliate and Associate programs

Description: This site is a great place to find an affiliate program that will work for different types of businesses. To access the Affiliate Programs main page, click the *Affiliate Programs Directory* link in the center of the page near the top.

For an overview of the information and resources offered at this site, click the *Site Map* link at the bottom of the page.

11.2 BOTS (USING, BUYING, CREATING)

BotSpot.com

Website: http://www.botspot.com/

Keywords: Intelligent Agents and Bots (using, buying, creating, etc.)

Description: Botspot.com is a website that provides information related to intelligent agents and bots. A bot is a software tool used to find and sort through data. The tool is commonly called agents and used in data mining. As websites and the information contained continue to grow, bots have become essential tools to categorize sites and find data.

The types of bots available and their uses are growing constantly. Bots are commonly used for searching, shopping, meta searches, newsgroup searches, tracking, web monitoring, news gathering, personal assistants, web development, file sharing, site management and more.

This site was listed because information about bots and their uses are going to become increasingly relevant to organizations doing business on the web.

11.3 CUSTOMER SECURITY

Better Business Bureau Online

Website: http://www.bbbonline.org/

Keywords: Reliability and Privacy Seal Programs

Description: Making customers feel secure about making a purchase from your website is step in the right direction. The BBB offers *Reliability* and *Privacy Seal* programs that are intended to make customers feel confident about purchasing from websites.

11.4 DEMOGRAPHIC INFORMATION (WEB USERS)

CyberAtlas

Website: http://cyberatlas.internet.com/

Keywords: Demographic Information (web users)

Description: Do you want to know who uses the web? Go to the Cyber Atlas website and scroll down until you see the Cyber Atlas navigation column on the left side of the page. Click on the *Archives* link. The archives page contains links to pages with articles on demographics, geographics, hardware, traffic patterns, advertising, retailing, small business and more.

The articles on this site are good. There is a lot of useful information that will help you understand who uses the web and why they use it.

11.5 DIRECT E-MAIL

Double Click

Website: http://www.doubleclick.com/us/

Keywords: E-mail Marketing Services

Description: Double Click is an established provider of e-mail marketing services. This company provides tools and services to plan, execute and analyze e-mail campaigns. Full-service and self-service options are available.

It also offers services related to campaign management, online advertising, database marketing and marketing analytics. To see a list of the services offered, click the *Site Map* link.

Optininc

Website: http://www.optininc.com/

Keywords: E-mail Marketing Services

Description: Optininc offers permission-based e-mail marketing services. With permission-based e-mail marketing services, the recipient signs up to receive e-mail related to a specific subject. Relevant information is then delivered to opt-ins. The attached advertising pays for the cost of the service. You can select lists by interest, occupation, subscription source and other criteria.

PostMasterDirect

Website: http://www.netcreations.com/

Keywords: E-mail Marketing Services

Description: PostMasterDirect provides e-mail list management, list brokerage, and deployment services. The company is a leading provider of opt-in e-mail marketing services. This firm maintains quality e-mail lists and can target e-mail-marketing campaigns to help you reach hundreds of audiences.

Yesmail

Website: http://www.yesmail.com/

Keywords: E-mail Marketing Services

Description: Yesmail provides permission-based e-mail marketing services. The company offers a variety of services to help you get results from an e-mail marketing campaign. The people who receive Yesmail promotions sign up to receive specific types of e-mail offers, which helps to improve response rates. This firm specializes in e-mail marketing for customer acquisition and retention.

The prices for these services are easy to understand. The firm also has options that enable you to send e-mail to a small audience.

11.6 E-MAIL LIST SEARCHES

Publicly Accessible Mailing Lists

Website: http://paml.alastra.com/

Keywords: E-mail List Search Site

Description: This is a great place to search for e-mail lists. The firm does not provide direct e-mail services. If you find a list you like, one of the direct e-mail services listed may be willing to set it up for you or find a similar list.

11.7 E-MAIL LIST TOOLS/SERVICES

GotMarketing

Website: http://www.gotmarketing.com/

Keywords: E-mail List Construction, Management and Utilization

Description: GotMarketing offers the Campaigner Suite, which is designed to make permission-based marketing fast and easy. If you want to collect e-mail addresses at your website to send information to, this is a service worth considering.

The Campaigner Suite gives you all the tools you need to collect and manage e-mail addresses. It also provides tools to construct and distribute e-mail newsletters. The sample newsletters that were constructed with the tools this company provides are impressive.

11.8 LEGAL ISSUES

John Marshall Law School

Website: http://www.jmls.edu/cyber/index/advert.html

Keywords: E-commerce-Related Laws and Regulations

Description: The John Marshal Law School website contains law review articles and case information related to doing business online. The website contains a significant amount of information and links but not much conclusive information.

11.9 WEB MARKETING INFORMATION

*Avant Marketer

Website: http://www.avantmarketer.com/

Keywords: Online Advertising and Marketing Articles (excellent)

Description: The Avant Marketer website has some impressive articles related to online advertising and marketing. To access the search feature, scroll down on the listed page and click a *Read Full Article* link. The article pages feature text search boxes where you can type in a search subject.

The articles on this site are excellent. They're well-written and concise. General statements are backed up with facts and figures. If you're considering an online advertising or marketing campaign, check out the articles on this site.

Circle Media

Website: http://www.bmcommunications.com/

Keywords: Web Marketing and Advertising Information

Description: This website contains useful information related to web advertising and marketing. To find information on this site, click *Click Here to Enter* then click the *Site Index & Marketing Online* link at the bottom of the page displayed.

Internet Marketing Info.com

Website: http://www.internetmarketinginfo.com/

Keywords: Internet Marketing Articles

Description: Internetmarketinginfo.com features a variety of articles related to Internet marketing and website design, construction, and promotion. The main categories are, building your website, making money, promoting your website, and tracking your progress. Each of the main categories have sub-categories you can select to view specific articles.

This site contains an array of useful articles related to doing business on the Internet. The articles are good, easy to access and easy to read.

Jupiter Direct (Jupiter Research)

Website: http://www.jupiterdirect.com/

Keywords: Web and E-commerce Strategic Reports and Briefings

Description: Jupiter Direct offers a variety of strategic reports and briefings related to the web and e-commerce. Jupiter Research is a leading source of information related to web business and related issues. This firm's reports aren't cheap, but if they specifically relate to a question or problem you're having, it could be well-spent money.

MarketingSherpa

Website: http://www.marketingsherpa.com/

Keywords: Marketing Case Studies and Publications

Description: The Marketingsherpa.com has a variety of web-based advertising and marketing case studies. To access the case studies, click the *Search Library* link in the top navigation bar.

Click on the *KnowledgeStore* link to view print publications related to online marketing subjects.

Wilson Internet Services

Website: http://www.wilsonweb.com/articles/

Keywords: Web Marketing Information, Website Design and Promotion, etc.

Description: The Wilsonweb.com articles page contains an assortment of web marketing information. The articles on this page are good. It also offers an assortment of E-books related to doing business on the web.

11.10 WEB MARKETING RESEARCH

eMediaResources

Website: http://www.emediaresources.com/

Keywords: Online Marketing Research Reports

Description: eMediaResources offers eMediaReports. The reports are related to competitor research and analysis, strategy analysis, industry-specific websites, directories, and more. eMediaResources' reports provide useful information that will help you develop a web marketing strategy.

11.11 WEB MARKETING TERMINOLOGY

E-commerce & Marketing Dictionary

Website: http://www.udel.edu/alex/dictionary.html

Keywords: E-commerce and Marketing Dictionary

Description: Need to find out what a web or Internet-related term or abbreviation means? This website is easy to use and quick loading. It enables you to search for definitions in alphabetical order. If you can't find what you need at this site, scroll to the bottom of the page and try one of the other resources listed.

Interactive Advertising Bureau

Website: http://www.iab.net/resources/glossary.asp

Keywords: Glossary of Interactive Advertising Terms

Description: The IAB website lets you search for definitions to terms and abbreviations related to web and interactive advertising.

It you have problems accessing the listed page, go to http://www.iab.net/ and type *glossary* in the search box and click go. Then click on one of the entries listed.

MarketingTerms.com

Website: http://www.marketingterms.com/

Keywords: Internet and Web-Related Marketing Terms and Definitions

Description: Marketingterms.com defines hundreds of terms and words related to web marketing. This is a great site. It's well organized and easy to use.

Website Development

12.1 CONTENT SERVICES

Idea Marketers

Website: http://www.ideamarketers.com/

Keywords: Articles and Information for Websites, etc.

Description: IdeaMarketers.com is a service where writers post articles that can be used in e-mail newsletters, websites, etc. In return for using information or an article, the user lists the source of the information and a related link (URL). Services like this give websites an affordable way to provide content. The downside, however, is that some of the readers will click on the related link and leave the host website.

12.2 CUSTOMER INCENTIVES

E-centives

Website: http://www.e-centives.com/

Keywords: Website Marketing Products and Services

Description: E-centives offers products and services to help you track customers, build databases, expand customer profiles, tailor offers, offer rewards, measure the success of promotions and more.

The services offered include strategic consulting and campaign management, user experience design and development services, analytics and data mining, and customer acquisition.

12.3 DATABASES

Searchdatabase.com

Website: http://searchdatabase.techtarget.com/

Keywords: Database Information and Resources

Description: Do you have a question about databases or related subjects? Searchdatabase.com is a leading source of information and resources related to databases. The site offers information related to specific products, industry news, vendor information, new products and technologies, related careers and more.

12.4 DOMAIN NAMES (REGISTRATION)

ICANN

Website: http://www.icann.org/registrars/accredited-list.html

Keywords: ICANN Accredited Domain Name Registrars

Description: The ICANN website lists ICANN accredited registrars. You can find an accredited registrar for all of the top-level domains at this site.

If you have problems finding this page, go to http://www.icann.org/ and scroll down until you see *Click Here for a List of Accredited Registrars* in the left column.

Network Solutions

Website: http://www.networksolutions.com/

Keywords: Domain Name Registration and Searches

Description: The Network Solutions website is a good place to register domain names. This firm has been in business a long time and its services are good. Some of the other registration services offered on the market, however, are less expensive.

12.5 DOMAIN NAMES (SELECTION)

DaySite

Website: http://www.daysite.net/

Keywords: Domain Name Selection Tips

Description: The listed website contains some tips to help you select a domain name. The information provided doesn't cover trademark issues, which you might want to consider when you select a domain name.

To access the naming information, click on *Naming Tips* in the left navigation column.

Network Solutions

Website: http://www.networksolutions.com/

Keywords: Domain Names Searches

Description: The Network Solutions website is a good place to access the Whois database to perform domain name searches. Go to the listed website and click the *Whois* link in the upper right-hand corner to access the database. (duplicate listing)

U.S. Patent & Trademark Office (USPTO)

Website: http://www.uspto.gov/

Keywords: Federal Trademark Searches

Description: The USPTO website contains a search trademarks (TESS) link that will take you to a page where you can search for registered trademarks, service marks, etc. If a name similar to the domain name you want to register is a registered U.S. Trademark or Servicemark, you might want to look into the related legalities. Legal advice is not within the scope of this guide.

Click the *Trademark* link on the listed page to access the page that lists the trademark search options.

12.6 PAYMENT PROCESSING INFORMATION (WEBSITE)

ChargeBackPrevention.com

Website: http://www.chargebackprevention.com/

Keywords: Charge-back and Fraud Prevention (credit cards)

Description: ChargeBackPrevention.com provides information, tips and guides related to credit card charge-backs and fraud. The information provided is intended to help site owners reduce charge-backs, fraud, and credit card processing fees.

12.7 PAYMENT PROCESSING (INTERNATIONAL WEBSITE SALES)

WorldPay

Website: http://www.worldpay.com/

Keywords: Multiple-Currency Payment Processing

Description: If you're selling products in multiple countries from your website, WorldPay is a service worth considering. This service enables you to accept 120 different currencies without having to keep track of currency exchange rates. Customers also benefit by being able to purchase products and services in a familiar currency. This service enables sites to accept credit cards, direct debits and other types of payments.

12.8 PAYMENT PROCESSING (WEBSITE CREDIT CARD SALES)

Electronic Payment Processing (EPP)

Website: http://www.epp-inc.com/

Keywords: Website Payment Processing Services

Description: EPP offers a service that enables you to make credit card sales from your website. The service offers secured processing of credit card payments. After a transaction is completed, you and the customer receive an e-mail notice with the amount, invoice number, order information, and where to ship the order.

EPP also offers swiped processing products and services to use in physical locations.

Glo-Bill

Website: http://www.globill-systems.com/

Keywords: Website Payment Processing Services

Description: Glo-Bill enables you to accept credit cards, online checks and per-minute dialer payments through your website. It also offers global telephone billing. Glo-Bill does not charge a setup fee. Instead, this firm charges a percentage of each sale. For an overview of these services, click the *Details* tab at the top of the page.

Paybutton

Website: http://www.paybutton.com/

Keywords: Website Payment Processing Services

Description: Paybutton offers a variety of products (levels of service) that enable web businesses to accept credit cards. The company offers basic-to-advanced solutions for websites. Paybutton's basic solutions are easy to set up and require minimal technical experience. Its advanced solution is a full e-commerce solution.

PayPal

Website: http://www.paypal.com/

Keywords: Website Payment Processing Services

Description: PayPal offers credit card and online check processing services for websites. This service enables a consumer or business with an e-mail address to securely, conveniently, and cost-effectively send and receive payments online. The company offers a variety of tools to help you process payments from your website.

PaySystems

Website: http://www.paysystems.com/

Keywords: Website Payment Processing Service

Description: PaySystems provides e-commerce solutions for Internet merchants Worldwide. This service enables websites to accept credit cards and online checks. It also offers an option for customers without a merchant account.

The features and prices of these services are competitive. PaySystems charges a setup fee to use its services, but the percentage of sales that it keeps is lower than many of the company's competitors.

VeriFone

Website: http://www.verifone.com/

Keywords: Payment Processing Services

Description: VeriFone is an established credit card processing company that provides payment processing terminals for stores that have a physical location. The information on its website indicates that most of what the company offers are products and services for physical stores.

VeriSign

Website: http://www.verisign.com/products/payment.html

Keywords: Website Payment Processing Services and Information

Description: VeriSign offers a variety of payment processing services. Its services enable websites to accept credit cards and online checks. The company has options for small-to-large websites. It also offers a recurring billing service that automatically bills customers for recurring charges such as memberships, partial payment options, etc. Its website features information to help you understand the process of collecting payments and the options the company offers.

12.9 PAYMENT & TRANSACTION PROCESSING (DIGITAL PRODUCTS)

ClickBank

Website: http://clickbank.com/

Keywords: Digital Product Sales

Description: Click Bank enables web vendors to sell digital products without the hassles. ClickBank makes the sale, pays the vendor and pays the affiliate.

The vendor gives ClickBank access to its product and selects an affiliate commission percentage. An Affiliate can then promote the product on its website and place a *Buy It at ClickBank* link on its site. Customers that want to buy the product, click the link and ClickBank takes care of the rest.

To find out more, click the *Register Products* link.

Vendor: The party that has a digital product to sell.
Affiliate: A business or individual that is promoting a product to receive a percentage of the sale price.

DigiBuy

Website: http://www.digibuy.com/

Keywords: Digital Products Sales

Description: DigiBuy enables you to sell digital products such as software, shareware, electronic information and data. This service enables you to build a secure web storefront to merchandise products, take orders online, process payments, and distribute digital products.

2CheckOut

Website: http://www.2checkout.com/index.html

Keywords: Digital Products Sales

Description: 2CheckOut offers an affordable service for websites that sell digital products and services. This service enables site owners to accept online checks and major credit cards. 2CheckOut does not distribute products. It simply processes the orders and routes the customer to where the product can be downloaded.

12.10 PHOTOGRAPHIC IMAGES

Corbis

Website: http://pro.corbis.com/default.asp

Keywords: Photographic Images (single and CDs)

Description: Corbis.com features some impressive photographs and collections that can be used for promotional materials. You will, however, have to sign up to view multiple photos in a specific category. Some of its photographs are royalty-free, while others involve rights and permissions.

Design Gallery Live

Website: http://dgl.microsoft.com/

Keywords: Photographic Images and Clipart

Description: Design Gallery Live enables you to search for photographic images and clipart. The firm also has sounds and motions that can be used on websites. I could not find a pricing page or related information. My best guess is that you can download and use the items free of charge.

You might want to check out its *Template Gallery*. You can access it from the navigation column on the left side of the page. This page contains templates for operations forms, brochures, various promotional materials and more.

IStock

Website: http://www.istockphoto.com/

Keywords: Photographic Images You Can Download

Description: Need a photographic image for your website? If so, iStock is an excellent place to look. When you sign up, you will receive two download credits. After you have used your free credits, each download will cost you 50 cents.

There are tens of thousands of photos on this site. You can search by category to find a photo that suits your specific needs.

12.11 WEB & INTERNET TERMINOLOGY

Netlingo

Website: http://www.netlingo.com/searchstation.cfm

Keywords: Internet, Web, and Chat room Terminology

Description: If you need to know what a word or term related to the Internet or web means, this site can help. You can search by category or keyword. You can also browse for definitions alphabetically.

12.12 WEBSITE ANALYSIS

WebSideStory

Website: http://www.websidestory.com/

Keywords: Website Analytics

Description: WebSideStory is a leader in outsourced web analytics. This company's HitBox services help businesses improve its websites and marketing efforts by providing actionable, real-time information about visitors and customers. It also offers StatMarket, which is information drawn from the collective surfing behavior of millions of users each day. StatMarket is a valuable resource for anyone interested in global Internet user trends.

12.13 WEBSITE DESIGN

All Graphic Design

Website: http://www.allgraphicdesign.com/

Keywords: Graphic Design and Development Resources

Description: Deezen.com is a good place to look for information and tips related to website development and graphic design. Its website features forums, software specific tips, software downloads, education/schools, graphic design techniques, graphic design resources, graphic design books, web design resources and more. This site has a lot of useful information and resources for website designers.

eFuse

Website: http://www.efuse.com/index.html

Keywords: Website Design Tips and Information

Description: eFuse offers useful information to help you start, plan, design, build and add to a website. This is a good site. It is reasonably easy to find what you need to know. For a quick overview of the site, click the *Site Map* link on the bottom of the page.

The Webby Awards

Website: http://www.webbyawards.com/main/

Keywords: Website Awards (top websites)

Description: The Webby Awards is a service that judges and selects winning websites in various categories. If you're trying to decide how to design or improve a site, this is a good place to look for ideas.

Web Pages That Suck

Website: http://webpagesthatsuck.com/

Keywords: Website Design Tips

Description: This site offers some critical evaluations of websites and design techniques. It contains information and examples to help you avoid common mistakes.

*Wilson Web

Website: http://www.wilsonweb.com/webmarket/

Keywords: Site Design Articles

Description: Wilson Web has search features that enable you to find articles related to website design. Use the *Search Our 8,000-plus Article Database* search box to find articles related to website design, doing business on the Web, etc.

You can also access articles by scrolling down the page and clicking on a sub-heading. When you click on a sub-heading, you're taken to a page with descriptions of related articles.

Web Style Guide

Website: http://www.webstyleguide.com/index.html

Keywords: Website Design Tips

Description: The Web Style Guide provides information related to website design. The site offers information related to process, interface design, site design, typography, editorial style, graphics and multimedia.

12.14 WEB SITE DEVELOPMENT & PLANNING

Builder.com

Website: http://builder.com.com/

Keywords: Website Development and Product Reviews

Description: CNET operates the Builder.com website, which contains a wealth of information related to software and hardware. The Product Review section is designed to help companies and site developers choose hardware and software.

Lynda.com

Website: http://www.lynda.com

Keywords: Website Development Applications, Training and Support

Description: Lynda.com is an information website that offers online training, CD-ROMs and books for popular website development applications. If you have a question or problem with a popular web development application, Lynda.com is a good place to look for help.

Webmonkey

Website: http://hotwired.lycos.com/webmonkey/

Keywords: Website Development Information

Description: Webmonkey offers useful information and resources related to building and maintaining websites. It features information related to authoring, design, multimedia, E-business, programming, backend applications, JavaScript, HTML, special characters, color codes, browsers, style sheets, Unix, etc. It's a great site that is updated frequently.

12.15 WEB SITE PERSONALIZATION

CRMDaily.com (customer relationship management)

Website: http://www.crmdaily.com/

Keywords: CRM and Personalization Information

Description: CRMDaily is an information website for customer relationship management professionals. It contains information on tools and techniques used to make websites functional for customers. Most of the information on this site is intended for medium-to-large sized businesses. Several of the articles listed, however, were relevant to anyone that wants to design an effective website. The *Next Step for Personalization* article grabbed my attention because it was direct and put the concept of personalization into perspective.

12.16 WEBSITE & ONLINE BUSINESS STRATEGY

Joscon Networks

Website: http://linz1.net/

Keywords: Online Business Tips, Websites, E-commerce, etc.

Description: The Joscon website contains information to help you develop a business plan, online business strategy and more. There are 2,000-plus pages of information on this site related to business and doing business on the web. If you have problems finding what you're looking for, click the *Site Map* button in the *Search This Site* box at the bottom of the page.

Net101

Website: http://www.net101.com/reasons.html

Keywords: Website Strategy Tips

Description: Net 101 provides basic tips that are worth considering if you're planning to do business on the web. The information provided is a good reminder of things that should be considered in a website strategy.

12.17 WEBSITE SURVEYS

The software and services available for website surveys are extensive. The listed services provide affordable options for small websites.

Feedback Today

Website: http://www.feedbacktoday.com/

Keywords: Website Surveys (simple and affordable)

Description: Feedback Today makes it easy to create and conduct online surveys. You can try this service and get your first 30 responses free. After 30 responses, you pay a recurring monthly fee to continue using this service.

Feedback Today has done a great job of making its website easy to use. Everything about it is user friendly.

Hosted Survey

Website: http://www.hostedsurvey.com/default.htm

Keywords: Website Surveys (intermediate-advanced)

Description: Hosted Survey offers intermediate to advanced levels of service. This service enables you to select fonts, colors, styles and backgrounds. You can also use your logo and customize the wording of prompts, buttons and messages.

The company offers a free 30-day trial, and its pricing information is tangible. It's relatively easy to understand what you'll get for your money. Many of the survey services reviewed offered limited pricing information.

SurveyForms

Website: http://www.surveyforms.net/

Keywords: Web Surveys (basic-intermediate)

Description: Survey Forms enables small website owners to conduct online surveys. This service is easy to use and affordable. The company offers different levels of service to suit the various needs of businesses. You can try its basic service free of charge. Surveys can be mailed to an e-mail list, posted on your website or hosted on its website.

Website Promotion

13.1 DOMAIN NAME REGISTRATION SITES

The following are registration services you can use to register domain names:

directNIC

domainit.com

domainvalet.com

easyspace.com

4domainnames.com

instant-domain.com

internicdomainnames.com

namesecure.lycos.com

NewDomainRegistrations.com

1-domain.com

101domain.com

parthe.net

register.com

register.com.sg

sitenames.com

13.2 WEBSITE PROMOTION INFORMATION (SEARCH ENGINES)

Advertising Secrets

Website: http://advertisingsecrets.com/

Keywords: Advertising and Marketing-Related Articles

Description: The Advertising Secrets website features an *Article* page with useful articles related to online advertising and marketing. The information is useful, easy to find and easy to read. The *Promote a Site link* on the top of the page takes you to a resource page with tools and services related to site promotion.

SitePoint

Website: http://www.sitepoint.com/

Keywords: Site Promotion and Construction

Description: SitePoint contains information and articles to help you promote and construct a website. Click on a subject link in the left column to access related articles. The articles are rated on a scale of 1-10 and various subjects are covered.

Spider Food

Website: http://www.spider-food.net/

Keywords: Site Promotion and Search Engine Tips, Forums

Description: The Spider Food website contains information related to site promotion and search engines. If can't find the information you need, join one of the site's forums and post your question. This is great site. It is easy to navigate and contains an abundant amount of useful information.

Spider Food provides information on concepts, keywords, page titles, meta tags, design/layout, framed sites, doorway pages, gateway pages, link popularity, theme engines, handling robots, monitoring rank, analyzing traffic, dynamic pages, layers/CSS, reference charts, spamming, site submission, website promotion and more.

The Internet Marketing Center

Website: http://www.marketingtips.com/tipsltr.html

Keywords: Internet Marketing Information Package

Description: The Internet Marketing Center offers an information package with information to help you market a website. It covers bulk e-mail and other methods used to sell products and increase website traffic. If bulk e-mail advertising is something you're willing to consider, you might want to take a look at its offer.

WebAdvantage.net

Website: http://www.webadvantage.net/default.htm

Keywords: Site Promotion and Marketing Articles

Description: The WebAdvantage archive page features numerous articles related to website marketing. It also offers website marketing services. To access the marketing information, click the *Marketing Tips* link at the top of the page. The

Marketing Tips page contains a group of links, which includes a link to the *Marketing Tips Archive*. Click it to access the archive.

E-mail Newsletter: You can sign up to receive a biweekly e-mail newsletter.

WebChicken

Website: http://www.wcresources.com/

Keywords: Website Development and Promotion Tools

Description: The WebChicken is a substantial resource for anyone wanting to develop or promote a website. There's a substantial amount of resources and information at this site. Subjects covered include planning a website, developing a product, writing copy for a site, building websites, e-commerce solutions, Internet marketing, promoting websites, search engine tips, and more.

It also offers a variety of free Internet classes.

13.3 WEBSITE PROMOTION SERVICES

Add Me, Inc.

Website: http://www.addme.com/index.htm

Keywords: Website and E-business Promotion

Description: Add Me offers a free service that enables you to submit your website to search engines (basic submission). It also offers professional submission services to 2,000 search engines and classifieds. Its website features information related to website promotion and the company offers a free e-mail newsletter with promotion tips and advice. For an overview of past issues, click the *Articles* link in the left column.

PositionAgent/Submit It

Website: http://www.positionagent.com/

Keywords: Search Engine and Directory Submission Service

Description: Position Agent and Submit It (originally two separate services) have been merged. The services offered are substantial and worth considering. For most websites, the submission services the company offers are adequate to get started. Site owners that want to establish or maintain high rankings will need to take additional steps to optimize their listings.

The links at the bottom of the page will take you to pages that provide information to help you get results with search engines. You'll also find tips to help you get other websites to link to yours.

Search Engine Forums

Website: http://searchengineforums.com/

Keywords: Directory of Search Engine Forums

Description: Search Engine Forums lists a variety of forums related to search engines. You can view questions and answers posted by various participants. There is a lot of useful information posted that will help you get results with search engines. To post a question, however, you'll have to sign up.

*Search Engine Watch

Website: http://searchenginewatch.com/

Keywords: Search Engine Information

Description: Searchenginewatch.com provides useful information that will help you get results with search engines. If you have a question or problem related to search engines, this is a good place to look for answers.

SelfPromotion.com

Website: http://www.selfpromotion.com/index.t

Keywords: Do-It-Yourself Website Promotion Resources

Description: SelfPromotion provides information and resources to help you pro-mote a website. The service works like shareware. If you like what you get, you can contribute what you think the service is worth. If you contribute within four weeks of setting up an account, your data will be maintained for a year. If you don't contribute, it will be deleted after four weeks.

13.4 WEBSITE PROMOTION SOFTWARE

Agent Web Ranking

Website: http://www.agentwebranking.com/

Keywords: Promotion Monitoring Software (search engine ranking)

Description: Agent Web Ranking monitors how your website is ranking on search engines. It automatically checks the listings of websites on search engines and provides customized ranking reports. Agent Web Ranking is global software that works with and uses all of the major search engines and directories. Its search engines library is updated within 72 hours in the event that a search engine changes the way it displays results.

PromotionalSoftware.com

Website: http://www.promotionalsoftware.com/

Keywords: Website Promotion Software

Description: Promotionalsoftware.com features Web Position Gold 2 promo-tional software. You can download and try a trial version. Web Position Gold 2 is a leading software product used to promote websites.

WordTracker

Website: http://www.wordtracker.com/

Keywords: Keyword Identification Software

Description: WordTracker identifies keywords to use when you're submitting a website to search engines. This service will help you identify the keyword combinations you should use. It will also help you understand the results you can expect with various search engines.

Using a service like the one offered by WordTracker will help you get higher rankings on search engines.

Marketing Associations

14.1 ASSOCIATION SEARCH SITES

ASAE (American Society of Association Executives)

Website: http://info.asaenet.org/gateway/OnlineAssocSlist.html

Keywords: Association Search Site

Description: If you need to find a specific type of trade association, the ASAE website is a good place to start. Simply type in a subject or keyword in the *Association Name Contains* search box and press go. This site also gives you the option of specifying categories and regions. It contains thousands of listings and is very functional.

The Trade Association Forum (U.K.)

Website: http://www.taforum.org/searchgroup.pl?n=500

Keywords: U.K. Trade Association Search Site

Description: If you need to find a U.K. trade association, this site is a good place to start. Follow the instructions at the top of the page to locate U.K. trade associations.

14.2 MARKETING

American Marketing Association (AMA)

Website: http://www.marketingpower.com

Keywords: Marketing Association

Description: The AMA is a professional society of marketers and market research executives. AMA is a leading organization that offers a variety of information and services for marketing professionals.

Books and Publications: This firm publishes the *Marketing News*, which is a member only biweekly newspaper. Its website features periodicals of interest to marketing professionals. You can access the publications page from any page on the site. It provides descriptions of various publications available.

Bookstore: http://ecommerce.ama.org/bookstore/ features an array of titles of interest to marketers. It offers a brief description of each title and makes it easy to place an order.

Direct Marketing Association (DMA)

Website: http://www.the-dma.org

Keywords: Direct Marketing Organization

Description: The DMA provides information and services to businesses interested in direct, database, and interactive global marketing. The DMA represents its member interests, promotes the DM industry, offers training, hosts networking events, etc.

Members: DMA members include catalog companies, direct mailers, Internet marketers and others that market to consumers and businesses.

Books and Publications: DMA offers a variety of books and publications.

Bookstore: http://www.the-dma.org/bookstore/cgi/bookstore The DMA bookstore features a variety of publications of interest to marketing and direct marketing professionals. It features books, CDs, cassettes, reports, etc.

Electronic Retailing Association (ERA)

Website: http://www.retailing.org

Keywords: Electronic Retailing Association

Description: The ERA is an international trade organization for companies that use electronic media to sell goods and services to the public.

Members: Members include television, radio, Internet retailers and back-end suppliers.

Books and Publications: The ERA offers a free e-mail newsletter.

Bookstore: http://www.retailing.org/facts/bookstore.html The ERA bookstore offers a variety of titles associated with electronic retailing and related subjects.

Marketing Research Association (MRA)

Website: http://www.mra-net.org

Keywords: Marketing Research Organization

Description: The MRA works to advance the opinion and marketing research profession. Its website is a good place to find information related to opinion and marketing research.

Members: Companies and individuals involved in any area of marketing research.

Books and Publications: The MRA website features a variety of publications related to opinion and market research.

Bookstore: Amazon Affiliate http://www.mra-net.org/docs/products_services/bookstore/index.cfm

Online Store: http://www.mra-net.org/ecom/showcategories.cfm Features videos, reports, publications, etc.

14.3 ONLINE RETAILERS

Shop.org

Website: http://www.shop.org/index.asp

Keywords: Online Retailer Organization

Description: Shop.org is a business organization for large online retailers. Shop.org provides a forum for online retailing executives to share information. This firm conducts workshops, local networking events, teleconferences, operates a retailer-only listserv, offers an annual members summit and publishes a weekly e-mail newsletter and its *State of Retailing Online Research Study*.

Shop.org membership is not cheap. It's primarily for established online retailers or individuals and companies that are serious about online retailing.

14.4 PRODUCT DEVELOPMENT & MANAGEMENT

Product Development & Management Association

Website: http://www.pdma.org/

Keywords: Product Development (by country/globally)

Description: The PDMA works to improve the effectiveness of people and organizations working to develop new products. This firm publishes *Visions* (a quarterly newsletter related to product development), *The Journal of Product Innovation Management* (bimonthly) and *The PDMA Handbook of New Product*

Development. Its website contains a lot of useful information. You can read articles from issues of *Visions* and search for related books.

14.5 TRADE SHOW SEARCH SITE

Trade Show Exhibitors Association

Website: http://www2.tsnn.com/

Keywords: Trade Show Search Page

Description: Looking for a specific type of trade show in a specific region? The TSEA trade show locator is a good place to start.

Periodicals

15.1 ADVERTISING RELATED

Advertising Age

Website: http://www.adage.com/

Keywords: Advertising News and Information

Description: Advertising Age is a print periodical for advertising professionals. It provides comprehensive weekly news related to the U.S. advertising business. Most of the articles and information relate to large advertisers and industry issues.

Advertising Age is available in print and online form.

Adweek & Adweek.com

Website: http://www.adweek.com/aw/index.jsp

Keywords: Advertising Periodical

Description: Adweek is a print periodical edited for ad agency executives. It covers creativity, client/agency relationships, successful global advertising strategies, the best creative work, new campaigns, etc. The magazine offers six regional issues. Its website features articles and related information.

Print and Online subscriptions are available.

Mediaweek

Website: http://www.mediaweek.com/mediaweek/index.jsp

Keywords: Media Periodical

Description: Media Week is a print periodical for media professionals. Media week covers media-related news, pricing news, cost comparisons, projected vs. actual ratings, demographics, trends, ad opportunities, etc. Its website features articles and related information.

Print and online subscriptions are available.

Media

Website: http://www.media.com.hk/world/core.htm

Keywords: Media Information for China, Hong Kong, Indonesia, Japan, Malaysia, Philippines, Korea, Singapore, Taiwan and Thailand

Description: Media.com lists numerous media resources for each listed country. The Media World page at http://www.media.com.hk/world/core.htm lists advertising agencies, Internet media, magazines and periodicals, newspapers, newspaper organizations, TV and radio stations, website development services and other media-related websites.

15.2 CATALOG RELATED

Catalog Age

Website: http://catalogagemag.com/

Keywords: Catalog-Related Periodical

Description: Catalog Age is a periodical for catalog direct marketers. The Catalog Age website contains numerous articles related to catalog sales, production, and marketing. You can review articles by subject. You can also sign up for related e-mail newsletters.

Catalog Success

Website: http://www.catalogsuccess.com/

Keywords: Catalog-Related Periodical, Related Articles

Description: Catalog Success.com contains useful information and articles related to catalogs and direct marketing. This company provides information related to catalog creation, production and printing, e-commerce, fulfillment, merchandising, database marketing, lists, media, and customer relationship management.

The site features a supplier search feature and an article archive. This firm charges for the articles offered.

15.3 COMPETITIVE INTELLIGENCE

Competitive Intelligence Magazine

Website: http://www.scip.org/news/

Keywords: Competitive Intelligence, Bimonthly Periodical

Description: CI Magazine is a bimonthly source of news and how-to advice related to competitive intelligence.

The Society of Competitive Intelligence Professionals (SCIP) publishes *CI Magazine* and the following.

Competitive Intelligence Review: A journal archive for peer-reviewed research and case studies.

SCIP's E-newsletter: Provides updates on important developments in the CI field and information about upcoming SCIP events.

CI Archive: Provides samples of CI articles but you have to be member to view full articles.

15.4 Customer Management & Support

Call Center

Website: http://www.callcentermagazine.com/

Keywords: Call Centers, Customer Support

Description: Provides information on call center-related hardware, software, and services. Call Center is commonly read by call center managers, IT managers, and other professionals involved with call centers and customer support departments. Its website contains useful information and articles.

15.5 Direct Marketing

Direct

Website: http://directmag.com/

Keywords: Direct Marketing Periodical

Description: Direct is a direct marketing periodical that is published 16 times per year. It covers postal and regulatory issues, creative topics, lists, customer relationship management, database marketing, direct mail, telemarketing, e-mail, direct response television and alternate media.

The Buyer's Guide enables you to search for resources commonly used by direct mail and catalog marketers.

15.6 DIRECT MAIL (DIRECT MAIL DESIGN & COPY)

*Inside Direct Mail

Website: http://www.insidedirectmail.com/

Keywords: Direct Mail Copy and Design (monthly newsletter)

Description: Inside Direct Mail is a monthly newsletter with information to help you get results with direct mail. Each month this publication's staff reads 3,000-plus pieces of direct mail to find the winners and the losers. As a subscriber, you'll have access to an archive of more than 150,000 mailing packages.

15.7 DISPLAY & MERCHANDISING PERIODICALS (RETAIL)

Creative (a magazine of promotion and marketing)

Website: http://www.creativemag.com/homepage.html

Keywords: Point of Purchase Displays, Trade Show Exhibits, etc.

Description: Creative is a bimonthly magazine for sales promotion and marketing executives. The focus of the magazine is point of purchase displays, trade show exhibits, and sales promotion programs.

Its website contains hundreds of listings related to displays, racks, and merchandising hardware. If you're operating a physical store, its website lists numerous products and services that may be of interest.

Point of Purchase (retail magazine)

Website: http://www.popmag.com/pointofpurchase/index.jsp

Keywords: Point of Purchase Periodical

Description: Point of purchase is a strategic marketing publication that covers POP advertising from the perspective of both brand marketers and retailers. It contains industry news, case studies, resources and more.

The POP website features an Online Buyer's Guide, which is a comprehensive resource of POP solutions for retailers.

15.8 E-PUBLICATIONS (SEARCH TOOL)

Electronic Journal Miner

Website: http://ejournal.coalliance.org/

Keywords: Electronic Publication Search

Description: The Electronic Journal Miner's website is a great place to search for e-mail periodicals and other electronic publications. It lists thousands of electronic periodicals related to thousands of subjects.

This site is an excellent place to find highly specialized electronic periodicals to advertise in or subscribe to.

15.9 GENERAL INDUSTRY PERIODICALS

**Primedia

Website:
http://www.mailcubed.com/news/primedia/category.asp?t=news

Keywords: Free E-mail Newsletters

Description: Primedia offers an array of free e-mail newsletters. You can subscribe to newsletters related to marketing and printing.

Marketing Titles Offered (free e-mail newsletters for marketers)

Catalog Age/Weekly newsletter for catalog marketers.
Direct Listline/Biweekly newsletter for finding and keeping up with marketing lists.
Direct Newsline/Daily newsletter for direct marketers.
Promo Xtra/Weekly newsletter for the promotion marketing industry.
The O&F Weekly Update/is for operations executives that sell directly through a catalog.

Red Herring

Website: http://www.redherring.com/

Keywords: Internet, E-commerce and Business

Description: The Red Herring covers issues related to innovation, technology, financial markets, technology-related companies, trends, etc.

15.10 IMPORT/EXPORT TRANSPORTATION

Commonwealth Business Media

Website: http://www.cbizmedia.com/prodserv/

Keywords: Transportation-Related Periodicals and Publications

Description: Need to find a service to get something somewhere? This site is a good place to start. The company offers transportation-related periodicals and publications.

To search for related periodicals and publications click the *Products and Services* link.

15.11 INTERNET & E-BUSINESS MARKETING

BtoB

Website: http://www.btobonline.com/

Keywords: Magazine for Marketing Strategists

Description: BtoB provides business-to-business marketers with information to help them investigate, analyze, understand, and implement e-technology strategies. The focus of BtoB is to provide top-level marketers with information related to various aspects of marketing. If you're marketing a business-to-business product or service in the U.S. or overseas, this publication is worth considering.

**Business 2.0

Website: http://www.business2.com/

Keywords: Internet Marketing, E-commerce and Related Issues

Description: Business 2.0 is a leading print periodical that covers an array of issues related to Internet businesses. Many of the articles cover issues that technology companies and related industries are facing. The magazine is insightful and enjoyable to read.

Its website contains articles from present and past issues, daily editorial features, and columns. Business 2.0 Live is a monthly series of panel discussions, which feature compelling personalities that discuss related subjects.

E-mail Newsletters: You can subscribe to the following from the Business 2.0 website.

Gizmos Weekly/weekly/New product reviews
Media Notes/weekly/What is and isn't working in digital media
What's Next/bimonthly/What's next inside silicone valley
Future Boy/newsletter/People and businesses that are going to remake the economy

Talent Monger/2 monthly/Career advice and recruiting tips
The Defogger/2 monthly/Perspective on trends, new products and hot players
Wireless Report/weekly/Wireless-related news and industry intelligence
Marketing Focus/weekly/News, trends, and campaign analysis, online and traditional
Daily Insight/Daily/Commentary on issues from technology to management
Tech Investor/Daily/Analysis of tech stocks
What's New at Business 2.0/monthly/The latest stories and columns

Context

Website: http://www.contextmag.com/

Keywords: Strategic Perspective on Technology Driven Changes

Description: Context is published every two months and commonly read by senior executives. The content relates to strategic planning in a business environment transformed by technology. Its website features articles from various issues.

Electronic Commerce World

Website: http://www.ecomworld.com/

Keywords: E-commerce Products, Services, etc. (monthly)

Description: Electronic Commerce World is a print periodical for middle-to-upper management. ECW covers electronic commerce implementations, financial EDI, electronic messaging, workflow automation, shipping, etc. Its website contains hundreds of links and articles related to e-commerce. Most of the information and products listed are of interest to medium and large sized organizations.

Fast Company

Website: http://www.fastcompany.com/homepage/

Keywords: Monthly Business Periodical (Internet businesses, strategy, marketing, etc.)

Description: Fast Company is a leading business periodical that contains interesting articles related to leadership, careers, strategy and innovation, human resources, Internet technology, marketing and branding, education and resources, sales and branding, etc. Fast Company is interesting and informative. Its website contains hundreds of useful links and articles of interest to marketers.

E-mail Newsletters (http://www.fastcompany.com/newsletter/)

The First Impression/Daily e-mail newsletter will give you a dose of forward thinking
Fast Take/Weekly e-mail newsletter with web-exclusive articles, event highlights, resources, and discussions
Fast Talk/E-mail newsletter that brings you the best of the Fast Talk Forums

Global Reach Express

Website: http://glreach.com/eng/ed/gre.php3

Keywords: Internet-Related News (International)

Description: Global Reach Express is a newsletter that covers Internet-related developments outside of the U.S. Topics covered include translation, localization, online populations, targeting online activity, website promotion techniques for international visibility, etc. It also offers a useful newsletter for individuals and companies interested in making sales abroad from their website.

*Line 56

Website: http://www.line56.com/

Keywords: E-business Technology, Strategy

Description: Line 56 is a leading source of global news and analysis on e-business technology and strategy. Topics covered include procurement, supply chain management, enterprise technology, content management, portals, e-markets, strategy and more.

Its website features links of interest to web marketers. Links include: magazines, related websites, web events, research and custom publishing, buyers guides and directories, and articles.

Revolution

Website: http://www.revolutionmagazine.com/

Keywords: Digital Business and Marketing (weekly periodical)

Description: Revolution is a weekly periodical that covers web marketing and web-related business issues. It contains news, analysis and case studies. Revolution is a U.K.-based publication that is becoming popular in the U.S.

15.12 LABELS (SYSTEMS & BUSINESS FORMS)

Business Forms, Labels & Systems

Website: http://www.bfls.com/

Keywords: Business Forms, Label Systems

Description: BFL&S is a periodical that provides information related to business forms, labels and related products. Its website contains a lot of useful information.

The *Article Archive* contains articles related to business forms, commercial printing, direct mail, e-commerce, marketing and sales techniques, promotional products and more.

15.13 MARKETING-RELATED PERIODICALS

American Marketing Association

Website: http://www.marketingpower.com

Keywords: Marketing Periodicals, Publications, and Reports

Description: To find the periodicals and publications available from the AMA website, select the *Site Map* link at the top or bottom of the page. Some pages do not have a *Site Map* link.

Once you've opened the site map page, click on *Publications* under the AMA Info sub-heading. It takes you to a page that lists and describes pages with periodicals, journals, and books. Some of the periodicals and journals offered by the AMA are listed below.

American Marketing Association (AMA) Periodicals

Marketing News (member publication): A biweekly newspaper, which is the official publication of the American Marketing Association. It contains news, analysis, and information of interest to marketers, researchers, and communicators.

Marketing Management: Marketing Management is a bimonthly print periodical edited for middle-to-senior-level marketing managers. It gives marketing executives insight on marketing practices and processes.

It also offers publications related to market research, international marketing, marketing health services, marketing services and marketing educators.

Brandweek (web information site)

Website: http://www.brandweek.com/brandweek/index.jsp

Keywords: Marketing Periodical

Description: Brandweek is a print periodical edited for marketers. Its website provides information on the publishing firm's print periodical and online subscription service. Brandweek covers marketer and retailer relationships, successful media strategies, agency/client relationships, global marketing, consumer trends, new campaigns, promotions, new product news, etc.

Print and online subscriptions are available.

Marketing Magazine (Canada)

Website: http://www.marketingmag.ca/index.cgi

Keywords: Canadian Marketing Magazine (information site)

Description: Marketing is a weekly print periodical that covers the Canadian marketing business. The firm also publishes *The Annual Marketing Awards Creative Book*, *Ad Agency Directory*, *Digital Marketing* (a sister publication), *Promo Marketing*, and *The PR Report*.

Promo Magazine

Website: http://www.promomagazine.com/

Keywords: Marketing-Related Trends, Issues and News

Description: Promo Magazine is a marketing periodical for marketing professionals at consumer product and service companies, retail chains, Internet businesses, marketing agencies, and supplier companies serving the promotion industry. Senior and middle-level marketing executives responsible for branding strategies primarily read it.

Its website contains a lot of interesting articles and information. It has a resource page (click the *Sourcebook* link) that enables you to search for suppliers of products and services commonly used by marketers. The *Research and Tools* link connects you to a search page where you can search through thousands of market research reports related to business, finance, communications, computers, IT, health care, industrial markets, Internet, manufacturing, etc.

You can sign up for a free subscription at its website.

Target Marketing

Website: http://www.targetonline.com/

Keywords: Direct Marketing Periodical

Description: Target Marketing is a print periodical for direct marketers. Target Marketing covers direct mail, telemarketing, space advertising, the web, direct response TV, using databases and lists effectively, acquiring new customers, up-selling and cross-selling to existing customers, fulfillment strategies and more.

Its website features links and information of interest to direct marketers.

Technology Marketing

Website: http://www.technologymarketing.com/mc/index.jsp

Keywords: Technology Marketing Periodical

Description: Technology Marketing is a print periodical for senior-level marketing executives in the technology industry. You can get subscription information at the listed address. TM provides in depth information related to marketing computers, software, Internet telecommunications, office equipment, etc. TM gives readers the insight they need to market products and services effectively.

15.14 MARKET RESEARCH

Quirk's Market Research Review

Website: https://www.quirks.com/subscribe/subscribe.asp

Keywords: Market Research, Case Studies, Technique Articles, etc.

Description: Quirk's Market Research Review is a print periodical that is published 11 times per year. It contains articles related to marketing research, case studies, technique, data use, etc. It also offers directories of research providers.

15.15 MARKETING SOFTWARE

Marketing Software Review

Website: http://www.schell.com/review/

Keywords: Marketing Software Review Periodical

Description: The Marketing Software Review is published monthly. It covers software for catalog order entry and fulfillment, database marketing and analysis, Internet order management, Internet customer service, manifesting, telemarketing, contact management, etc.

Most of the software covered is for small-to-medium-sized operations.

15.16 MEDIA SEARCH

Gebbie Press

Website: http://www.gebbieinc.com/

Keywords: Media Search Site

Description: The Gebbie Press website enables you to search for the websites of newspapers, TV stations, radio stations and magazines. The magazine search tool enables you to search for related periodicals by subject. Selecting a subject displays a list of related periodicals. Click on a periodical and you are connected to its website.

Magazine and periodical websites are generally good sources of related information. After finding these sites, you may want to bookmark them or save them as favorites for easy access.

15.17 NEWSPAPER SEARCHES

Tilpon

Website: http://www.tilpon.com/

Keywords: International Newspaper Location Website

Description: The Tilpon website enables you to locate newspapers and related websites in countries around the world. If you can't find the news you need in English, you can use one of the language translation sites listed in the International Business section to translate it.

15.18 PERIODICAL INFORMATION (MEDIA SEARCHES)

American Journalism Review (AJR)

Website: http://www.ajr.org/

Keywords: Periodical Searches/Media Searches

Description: If you need to find an industry-specific periodical or general-media source, this site is a good place to start. It lists newspapers, magazines, television networks, radio stations and more.

Media Finder

Website: http://www.mediafinder.com/

Keywords: Periodical and Newsletter Searches

Description: Media Finder is a good place to locate a specific type of periodical, newsletter or catalog. The Media Finder website enables you to search for periodicals, newsletters and catalogs related to hundreds of subjects.

You'll have to subscribe to view full listings.

Ulrich's Periodical Directory

Website: http://www.ulrichsweb.com/ulrichsweb/

Keywords: Global Periodical Search (global)

Description: The Ulrich's Periodical Directory website is a comprehensive source of information on serials (periodicals) throughout the world. If you're interested in doing business in a foreign country, this is a good place to find specialized information sources.

You'll have to sign up to use this site. The company offers a limited trial option that enables you to try this service for a limited period.

NewsLink

Website: http://newslink.org/

Keywords: National and International Media Companies

Description: Newslink.org is a good place to find industry-specific periodicals or general media sources. Its website enables you to search for media-related sources throughout the world. It lists magazines, newspapers, and radio/TV stations.

A limited number of magazines were listed in some of the categories I searched.

15.19 PRODUCT DEVELOPMENT & MANAGEMENT

Product Development & Management Association (PDMA)

Website: http://www.pdma.org/

Keywords: Product Development Newsletter and Related Publications

Description: The PDMA publishes *Visions Magazine* (quarterly), which is a periodical related to new product development. PDMA disseminates research findings through *The Journal of Product Innovation Management*, which is published six times per year. It also offers *The PDMA Toolbook for New Product Development* (John Wiley & Sons, 1996), which covers related developments and insights.

15.20 SALES (SALES FORCE)

Sales and Marketing Management

Website: http://www.salesandmarketing.com/salesandmarketing/index.jsp

Keywords: Sales and Marketing Professionals, Personnel Management Issues

Description: SMM is a periodical for sales and marketing professionals. It contains articles of interest to help sales and marketing professionals get results. It keeps them informed about various issues and events related to their profession.

15.21 SUPPLY CHAIN MANAGEMENT (SOFTWARE)

IDII (Industrial Data & Information, Inc.)

Website: http://www.idii.com/esn/

Keywords: Supply Chain Software Newsletter (bimonthly)

Description: If you're looking for information related to supply chain management software, this is good place to start. Its website is a substantial source of information on software used to manage supply chain operations.

Scroll down the page to view a list of past issues.

It also offers white papers, a book catalog, a resource page, reports, and more.

15.22 TRADE SHOW INFORMATION

Tradeshow Week

Website: http://www.tradeshowweek.com/

Keywords: Trade Show Information, Searches and Related Articles

Description: Tradeshow Week is a print periodical for trade show executives. The firm also publishes the *Tradeshow Week's Buyers Guide*, which lists related vendors, services and information. If you're interested in participating in trade shows, check out its website. There is a lot of information and resources on this site.

Its website lists related publications and enables you to search for trade shows, related products, and services.

15.23 E-MAIL NEWSLETTERS (MISCELLANEOUS)

BotSpot

Website: http://www.botspot.com/

Keywords: Intelligent Agents and Bots (bimonthly newsletter)

Description: Botspot.com is a website that provides information related to intelligent agents and bots. A bot is a software tool used to find and sort through data. The tool is commonly called an agent and used in data mining. As websites and the information they contain proliferate, bots have become essential tools to help categorize sites and find data.

If you need more information related to bots, you can find it at the BotSpot website or sign up for the site's bimonthly newsletter.

15.24 MISCELLANEOUS NEWSLETTERS

CRM Weekly (customer relationship management)

Website: http://www.dmnews.com/cgi-bin/index.cgi

Keywords: Weekly e-mail newsletter that covers database and CRM Marketing.

DM News—iMarketing News Daily

Website: http://www.dmnews.com/cgi-bin/index.cgi

Keywords: Free daily e-mail newsletter that covers direct marketing, e-commerce and Internet marketing.

Sam Magazine (free e-mail)

Website: http://www.sammag.com/index.cfm

Keywords: Sales, Advertising, Marketing, Free E-mail Publication

Description: The Sam Magazine is a free e-mail magazine for advertisers and marketers. The Sam Magazine website contains articles and information of interest to marketers.

The Internet Times

Website: http://glreach.com/eng/ed/it.php3

Keywords: Internet Newsletter/Technology and Global Marketing

Description: The Internet Times covers Internet technology advances and how they relate to global marketing.

15.25 U.K. MARKETING PUBLICATIONS

Haymark Publishing publishes the following U.K. publications. More information about each can be found at http://www.brandrepublic.com/shop/ Its website also lists other periodicals and guides of interest to companies and individuals marketing in the U.K.

Brand Republic

Website: http://www.brandrepublic.com/shop/

Keywords: Marketing, Advertising and Media

Description: *Brand Republic* is a leading periodical that covers issues, news, and events related to the marketing, advertising, and media industries.

Campaign

Website: http://www.brandrepublic.com/magazines/campaign/index.cfm

Keywords: Advertising, Marketing and Media (U.K.)

Description: *Campaign* is Britain's leading magazine for the advertising, marketing, and media sectors. It contains news and related articles.

Marketing (U.K.)

Website: http://www.brandrepublic.com/magazines/marketing/index.cfm or http://www.marketingmagazine.co.uk

Keywords: Marketing Periodical (U.K.)

Description: *Marketing* is a weekly marketing periodical. It contains articles and information related to marketing in the U.K.

PR Week

Website: http://www.prweek.com/

Keywords: Public Relations Periodical (U.K.)

Description: *PR Week* is a weekly periodical for the U.K. public relations industry. It covers business news related to all aspects of the public relations industry.

Publications

16.1 Advertising, Marketing, and Media Directories

Adweek Directory

Website: http://www.adweek.com/

Keywords: Advertising Directory

Description: The *Adweek Directory* provides information related to advertising agencies, public relations firms, media buying services, and specialty advertising shops. The listings include contact information, industries served, number of employees, year founded, billings, billings by medium, fee income, personnel/titles, accounts, parent company and subsidiaries.

To locate information on directories, click *Search Directories* in the left navigation column. The link takes you to a page that lists related directories. For more information, click on a specific directory title.

Bacon's (media directories)

Website: http://www.bacons.com/

Keywords: Media Directories/Media Source Internet

Description: Bacon's is a publisher of media sources. The company offers a variety of media-related publications. Its *Media Source Internet* lets you search for media resources online. You will, however, have to register to use it and your free trial only lasts two days.

Brandweek Directory

Website: http://www.adweek.com/

Keywords: Brand Directory

Description: The *Brandweek Directory* provides information on over 6,200 brands. Listings are organized by brand name with marketer, personnel, lead agency and media expenditure data. The listings feature marketer address, telephone, fax, URL, annual media expenditure, parent company, and lead advertising agency.

To locate information on directories, click *Search Directories* in the left navigation column. The link takes you to a page that lists related directories. For more information, click on a specific directory title.

Media Directory

Website: http://www.adweek.com/

Keywords: Media Reference Directory

Description: The *Mediaweek Directory* focuses on media companies in top markets. It covers radio, broadcast TV, cable TV, daily newspapers, consumer magazines, trade magazines, networks, syndicators, sales representatives, multi-media holding companies, trade associations and rating organizations.

To locate information on directories, click *Search Directories* in the left navigation column. The link takes you to a page that lists related directories. For more information, click on a specific directory title.

IQ Directory

Website: http://www.adweek.com/

Keywords: Interactive, New Media Marketing

Description: The *IQ Directory* profiles 2,200 interactive agencies, web developers, brand marketers, online media, CD-ROM developers, POP/kiosk designers, multimedia creative companies, etc.

To locate information on directories, click *Search Directories* in the left navigation column. The link takes you to a page that lists related directories. For more information, click on a specific directory title.

16.2 BRANDING

BrandChannel.com (produced by InterBrand)

Website: http://www.brandchannel.com/start.asp

Keywords: Branding-Related Books Reviewed

Description: *BrandChannel.com* offers a book review section, e-mail newsletter, articles and more. If you want to find out more about building or improving a brand, this is a good place to start.

The book review section of this website is substantial. It features reviews for numerous branding-related titles.

16.3 GOVERNMENT INFORMATION

National Technical Information Service (NTIS)

Website: http://www.ntis.gov/

Keywords: Government Information Search Site

(search for over 750,000 publications)

Description: Publications like the *U.S. Industry & Trade Outlook* and the *Statistical Abstract of the United States* can be found and ordered at the listed website. Many publications can be downloaded directly from the site. I used the search mechanism for a while and wasn't real impressed. It is, however, sufficient to find common government publications.

Sample Search Results: I entered *marketing* and *computers* in the NTIS advanced search feature and 7702 results were found. After the first page, the listed results were very relevant. The second page listed reports on computer-related exports to numerous countries.

16.4 IMPORT/EXPORT

Directories of U.S. Importers & Exporters (Piers Publishing Group)

Website: http://www.pierspub.com/ImpExp.htm

Keywords: Directories of U.S. Importers and Exporters

Description: *The Directories of U.S. Importers & Exporters* contain over 28,000 individuals and organizations involved in the U.S. import/export industry. The directories contain information to help you determine the value and volumes associated with various businesses. The directories also contain information related to broker and transportation service providers, detailed commodity descriptions, SIC codes and more.

16.5 IMPORT/EXPORT TRANSPORTATION

The Transportation Telephone Tickler

Website: http://www.pierspub.com/tickler.htm

Keywords: Transportation Supplier Information Directory

Description: *The Transportation Telephone Tickler* provides the names, addresses, telephone/fax numbers and personnel titles for 24,000 transportation services and suppliers in the U.S., Canada, Caribbean and parts of Latin America.

16.6 INTERNATIONAL REFERENCE

Nations of the World

A Political, Economic & Business Handbook

ISBN 1-891482-87-4 soft cover
ISBN 1-891482-88-2 hard cover

Website: www.greyhouse.com

Keywords: Country Information

Description: *Nations of the World* includes profiles of 228 nations around the world. It contains political, economic, and business information. It also features official country name(s), ruling parties, language, population, unemployment, and inflation figures.

Country profiles include detailed historical information, political structure and parties, population, labor market, media trade, industry, agriculture, and energy-related information.

Business travelers can find information about time zones, banking practices, entry requirements, dress codes, climate, health issues, hotels, working hours, recommended travel procedures, contact numbers and websites for hotels, travel information, and chambers of commerce.

For more information go to the listed page and click titles in the top navigation bar. You'll see Nations of the World listed in the business section.

16.7 INTERNET RELATED

Netlingo

Website: http://www.netlingo.com

Keywords: Internet and Web Terminology

Description: *Netlingo* covers 3,000-plus Internet and web-related terms and words. It also includes 1,200 chat acronyms. If you need to know about web-related terminology, this book is a good place to start

16.8 MARKET RESEARCH

Green Book
(New York AMA Communication Services)

Website: http://www.greenbook.org/

Keywords: Market Research and Focus Group Directories

GreenBook Worldwide Directory of Marketing Research Companies and Services
GreenBook Worldwide Directory of Focus Group Companies and Services

Description: The GreenBook Publications are leading marketing research and focus group reference publications. Each directory contains extensive listings of related companies and services. The company offers a sample of the information contained in each publication at its website.

Esomar

Website: http://www.esomar.nl/index.htm

Keywords: International Market Research Publications

Description: Esomar is a world association for opinion and marketing research professionals. The publications page lists the Esomar Publications. If you're interested in buying one of its publications, you might want to order it through Amazon.com or another bookseller. Esomar is located in the Netherlands, so ordering directly from the organization may not be practical.

16.9 MARKETING TERMINOLOGY

Dictionary of Marketing Terms

Website: http://www.marketingpower.com

Keywords: Dictionary of Marketing Terms

Description: *The Dictionary of Marketing Terms* is an AMA Publication (American Marketing Association). It's an excellent reference guide that will help you understand marketing terminology. It contains a lot of useful information.

To find the periodicals and publications available from the AMA website, select the *Site Map* link at the top or bottom of the page. Some pages do not have a *Site Map* link. You might have to click through some pages to find one.

Once you've opened the site map page, click on *Publications* under the AMA Info sub-heading. It takes you to a page that lists and describes pages with periodicals, journals, and books.

16.10 PRODUCT DEVELOPMENT

Product Development & Management Association

Website: http://www.pdma.org/bookstore/

Keywords: Product Development and Management Book Reviews

Description: The PDMA bookstore offers reviews of popular titles related to product development and management. If you're developing or improving a product, the PDMA website is a good place to look for useful information.

Books reviewed are categorized as newest, classics, best practice, process and strategy, organization and teams, cycle time, tools and techniques, industries and topics.

16.11 PUBLICATION SEARCH (GLOBAL)

Bowker's Global Books in Print

Website: http://www.globalbooksinprint.com/

Keywords: Book Search Site (global)

Description: The Bowker's Books in Print website is a good place to do an extensive search for available publications. This is a great place to find a publication related to a foreign country or specific subject.

You'll have to sign up for a courtesy trial to use the search features on this site.

Software

17.1 ADVERTISING PLANNING

AdCracker

Website: http://www.adcracker.com/

Keywords: Ad Design and Copy Writing/Tips and Interactive CD

Description: The AdCracker website features AdBasics, AdCreative and AdManagement pages that contain tips and information. The AdCracker website works to stimulate creativity and provides practical information.

The AdCracker CD is a tool to help people design ads, write copy for ads, and manage advertising and marketing-related activities.

Advertising Plan Pro (Palo Alto software)

Website: http://www.paloalto.com/index.cfm

Keywords: Advertising Planning Software

Description: Advertising Plan Pro has features to help you create an integrated marketing communications plan, centralize individual and group project efforts, clarify market segmentation, develop a competitive analysis, match your plan and budget, clarify your corporate strategy, evaluate results, etc. The formatting features will help you produce visuals, format your marketing budget and expense calculations in tables, illustrate with charts and graphs, and more.

Its website enables you to review product features.

17.2 BUSINESS PLANNING

Business Plan Pro/standard & premier (Palo Alto software)

Website: http://www.paloalto.com/

Keywords: Business Planning Software

Description: Palo Alto Software offers Business Plan Pro in standard and premier editions. Business Plan Pro provides over 400 sample business plans and the Easy Plan Wizard to get you started. It also has help and support features, easy to use tables, a built in graphic forecaster to help you forecast your sales graphically, and formatting features that merge text, tables, and charts automatically and create a table of contents. It integrates with other programs, allows you to import from QuickBooks, export to MS Word, MS Excel, PDF and HTML.

The premier edition adds collaboration tools to help you work efficiently and effectively with your team. It also enables you to combine different parts of existing plans. It includes features for expanded sales forecasting, personnel planning, profit and loss statements and enhanced cash flow management.

Its website gives you a thorough understanding of what you're getting. Simply click the product features link on the separate product pages.

OfficeReady Business Plans

Website: http://www.templatezone.com/

Keywords: Business Planning Software

Description: OfficeReady Business Plans is business planning software with features to help you develop a traditional or Internet business plan and create presentations. It includes ready to use examples from a variety of industries, integrates with Microsoft Word, Excel and PowerPoint, and includes predefined templates.

To access information about this product, click *Business Plans* in the Business Solutions column.

Plan Write (BRS Inc.)

Website: http://www.brs-inc.com/products.asp

Keywords: Business Planning Software (standard and expert editions)

Description: BRS Inc. offers Plan Write business planning software. Plan Write enables you to benefit from the knowledge of over 40 business experts, make your plan compelling and unique, calculate complex financial projections and more. Its website provides information about features and offers testimonials. The services tab will take you to a page where you can select case studies related to business planning, strategy and marketing.

Plan Write Expert enables you to have your plan reviewed by a business-planning expert that will provide insight and direction.

17.3 CATALOG MANAGEMENT

The Guide to Catalog Management Software

Website: http://www.schell.com/guide/

Keywords: Catalog Management Software, Order Processing and Fulfillment

Description: The Guide to Catalog Management Software and its companion volume, Choosing and Using Catalog Management Software provides information to help you choose the appropriate software. Solutions covered are of interest to companies that take orders by mail, phone, fax, or electronic commerce. The guides aren't cheap but if you're going to spend a substantial amount on a catalog, order processing, or fulfillment application, it might be money well spent.

17.4 COMPETITIVE INTELLIGENCE SOFTWARE

Knowledge Works

Website: http://www.cipher-sys.com/

Keywords: Competitive Intelligence Software

Description: Knowledge Works is designed for use with Microsoft Exchange/Outlook or Lotus Notes. It enables you to store information about competitors inside file cabinets with automation features to help you categorize, index, search, alert, monitor and subscribe to information, which is delivered by e-mail. You set up profiles and receive daily news and alerts to competitor moves. It has features to help you collaborate with colleagues, determine how the collected information should be handled, and determine how, when, and who should handle various tasks.

17.5 CUSTOMER SERVICE (WEBSITE SOFTWARE)

RightNow

Website: http://www.rightnow.com/

Keywords: Website Customer Service Software

Description: RightNow has become an industry leader in customer service software for websites. The company offers a multi-channel, customer-driven eService suite that helps companies improve the quality and responsiveness of their customer service operations.

17.6 DATABASE PRODUCTS (CUSTOMER INFORMATION MANAGEMENT)

Group 1 Software

Website: http://www.g1.com/

Keywords: Marketing Automation/Customer Data Management (high-end)

Description: Group 1 Software offers data quality, marketing automation, customer communications management and direct marketing software solutions. The company offers quality, high-end products to help you manage data, customer communications and direct marketing campaigns.

17.7 EXPORT SOFTWARE

Shipping Solutions

Website: http://www.shipsolutions.com/index.html

Keywords: Export Document Software

Description: Shipping Solutions offers software to help you prepare export documents. This company's software makes it easy for inexperienced exporters to complete export documents. It will also help you minimize errors and monitor shipping expenses.

The company offers different solutions to serve the needs of large and small exporters.

17.8 INTERNET & WEB STRATEGY

Web Pro Strategy (Palo Alto software)

Website: http://www.paloalto.com/

Keywords: Website Strategy Software

Description: Web Strategy Pro will help you organize a site strategy, analyze your market, compete in your industry, plan your implementation, understand costs and benefits, and more. Its website does a good job of describing the various features offered.

After reviewing the features of this software, it seems like a good product for the price.

E-marketing Suite

Website: http://www.templatezone.com/

Keywords: eMarketing Planning Analysis, and Forecasting

Description: eMarketing is a software package that works with MsOffice. The eMarketing Suite includes planning and sales forecasting tools, and eMetrics to measure web-based marketing. The suite is intended to help you quickly and professionally develop a detailed e-marketing plan with a thorough sales forecast, expense budget, contribution margin statement and more.

Click on *eMarketing* in the Business Solutions column or drop-down list at the top of the page.

17.9 LOGO SOFTWARE

The Logo Creator

Website: http://www.thelogocreator.com/

Keywords: Logo Creation Software

Description: The Logo Creator website features different versions of logo creation software. Each version comes with ready to use logos that you can modify.

17.10 MAILING LIST MANAGEMENT

Group 1 Software

Website: http://www.g1.com/

Keywords: Mailing List Management Software (high-end)

Description: Group 1 Software offers software that validates, corrects, matches and standardizes address data. It eliminates duplicate records and presorts mailings for the highest attainable postal discounts from the USPS. It utilizes the most current address data by tracking customers moves via the USPS fast forward change of address system. The company also offers an international version that validates addresses for over 220 countries and dependencies.

Melissa Data

Website: http://www.melissadata.com/

Keywords: Mailing List Software

Description: Melissa Data offers an array of mailing list and related software. The company offers medium-to-high-end applications for businesses that do a substantial amount of direct mailing. If you use or manage large mailing lists, the wide selection of software the company offers is worth considering. Many of the solutions offered give you an option to try it free or at minimal cost.

17.11 MAIL ORDER & E-COMMERCE

Response by CoLinear Systems

Website: http://www.colinear.com/

Keywords: Mail Order and E-commerce Software

Description: CoLinear Systems offers Response, which is a direct commerce and fulfillment system. Response is a reliable Windows-based application.

Response provides a wide range of integrated services including order processing, real-time customer service, inventory allocation and control, customer and order management, sales and media analysis, streamlined product fulfillment, electronic credit card processing, a networked fax server, comprehensive management reporting and more.

17.12 MARKETING MANAGEMENT

Marketing Management Analytics (MMA)

Website: http://www.mma.com/index.asp

Keywords: Marketing, Sales, and Industry Solutions (high-end)

Description: MMA offers a variety of software solutions for marketers. The company offers products related to marketing mix analysis, advertising effectiveness, brand planning and forecasting, impact of pricing actions, consumer promotion effectiveness, media scheduling, market structure, and competitive interaction analysis. The firm also offers sales and industry solutions.

The products and solutions offered by MML are high-end solutions for medium-to-large-sized businesses.

Aprimo Marketing

Website: http://www.aprimo.com/

Keywords: Enterprise Marketing Management Software (high-end)

Description: Aprimo Marketing offers a web-based software application that helps you manage and measure your marketing investment. It helps you implement marketing campaigns and understand which efforts are producing results.

17.13 MARKETING PLANNING

Marketing Plan Pro

Website: http://www.paloalto.com/ps/

Keywords: Marketing Plan Software/Standard and Premier Versions

Description: Marketing Plan Pro will help you create a marketing plan to find customers, raise awareness, and increase sales. It features 70-plus sample plans, works for different types of businesses, and enables you to add graphics and charts from other applications.

The Premier version includes the features listed above plus features to help you collaborate with a team. It also enables you to create a marketing plan template and save your plan as a template. It has additional charting, tracking, and forecasting-related features and enables you to import and combine multiple marketing plans.

OfficeReady Marketing Plans

Website: http://templatezone.com/

Keywords: Marketing Plan Software

Description: Office Ready Marketing Plans helps users create marketing plans for developing and running a business. The software has features that help you develop a marketing plan with a sales forecast, expense budget, and a contribution margin statement. You can choose from marketing effectiveness measures, competitive evaluations, and pricing analyses to ensure that plans are appropriate. It also has features to help you determine the value of customers, assess acquisition costs of campaigns, predict mailing list growth and more.

Click on *Marketing Plans* in the Business Solutions column or drop-down list at the top of the page.

Planned Marketing Software

Website: http://www.plannedmarketing.com/index.html

Keywords: Product or Service Analysis Software

Description: Planned Marketing Software will help you analyze a product or service. It gives you insight on locating new customers, improving an existing product or service, and creating a market analysis. It will help you find a new product or service, find new methods of distribution, test market a product or service, write advertising copy, create a competitive analysis and more.

Planned Marketing Software is inexpensive and has numerous features.

Plan Write for Hi-Tech Marketing (BRS Inc.)

Website: http://www.brs-inc.com/products.asp

Keywords: Marketing Plan Software for Hi-Tech Businesses

Description: *Plan Write for Hi-Tech Marketing* comes with a tactical guide to help you develop collateral, manage trade shows, and more. It will help you forecast budgets and timetables with pre-populated expenses, checklists, and milestones. You also receive an integrated hi-tech marketing book that provides specific techniques, terminology and focus stories. Your marketing strengths are automatically identified and illustrated graphically and through written analysis. Its testimonial page is substantial.

Click on the *Products* tab at the top of the page to locate product information.

Plan Write for Marketing (BRS Inc.)

Website: http://www.brs-inc.com/products.asp

Keywords: Marketing Planning Software

Description: *Plan Write for Marketing* will help you identify your market, document your strategy, prepare a budget, produce documents and execute your marketing plan. Its website features a product demonstration so you can get an idea of what you'll get for your money. Its testimonial page is substantial.

For an overview of products, click on the *Products* tab at the top of the page.

Ultimate Marketing Calculator

Website: http://templatezone.com/

Keywords: Marketing and Marketing Plan Analysis Software

Description: The Ultimate Marketing Calculator helps you analyze marketing strengths and marketing plans. The software features 38 marketing worksheets to help you make precise marketing calculations. It will help you compute the value of customers, calculate acquisition costs by promotional campaigns, calculate return on customer accounts, and calculate new economy metrics such as e-mail return on investment, e-mail sales forecasts, and website traffic.

To locate this product, click *Marketing Plans* in the Business-Solutions column or drop-down list. On the Marketing Plans page, click *All Products* in the left navigation column.

17.14 MARKET RESEARCH (ONLINE)

World Opinion

Website: http://www.worldopinion.com/tools.html

Keywords: Online Market Research Software and Services

Description: The World Opinion reference page lists products and services used to do market research online. It has a link to the WorldOpinion Bookstore, which provides information on marketing and research-related titles. It also contains links to research resources and related associations. Click the *Reference* link in the top navigation bar to access this page.

17.15 MARKETING STRATEGY

Business Insight (BRS Inc.)

Website: http://www.brs-inc.com/

Keywords: Strategic Planning Software

Description: Business Insight is strategic planning software that will help you develop a strategy to market a product or service. BI has received good reviews from substantial sources. It contains business models of strategy experts that will help you incorporate their expertise into your marketing strategy. It will help you structure strategic planning, promote creative thinking, identify variables that could impact your strategy and forecast the outcome of your strategic decisions. BI isn't cheap.

Click the *Business Insight* link on the listed page for more information. You can also view short descriptions of its products by clicking the products link at the top of the page.

17.16 MERCHANDISING SOFTWARE

AAXEOM

Website: http://www.aaxeom.com/

Keywords: Merchandising Software (website)

Description: ProfitPro Generator is website merchandising software. ProfitPro Generator is available with merchandising, visualization, customer profiling and call center modules. The merchandising module enables a non-technical staff to control which products are viewed under predetermined circumstances. The Visualization module presents multiple product images together in a logical scene. The customer profiling module delivers product recommendations, personally relevant content, and targeted promotions in real-time by capturing and combining customer browsing and profile data. The call center module provides customer service representatives access to a client's mix, match, and view sessions, which enables them to better serve customers and answer questions.

The visualization module is available as a stand-alone module or can be used with other modules.

AAXEOM

Website: http://www.aaxeom.com/

Keywords: Website Visualization Software (high-end)

Description: AAXEOM offers Pixel Merge, which is visualization software that helps customers visualize what is being offered at a website. Pixel Merge enables web customers to mix, match, and view how products look together. Websites that sell fashion apparel, home decorating products, cosmetics, jewelry, or products that visually complement other products, could benefit from this type of product.

Its website provides examples of how Pixel Merge can be utilized to help sell various products.

17.17 PRICING

Making Your Price Sell

Website: http://www.sitesell.com/

Keywords: Pricing Software

Description: Making Your Price Sell is an affordable solution to help you price products. Its website provides a good overview of what its product can do and explains some basic facts about pricing.

Scroll to the bottom of the page to see short descriptions of the various products the company offers.

Plan Write for Pricing

Website: http://www.brs-inc.com

Keywords: Pricing Software

Description: Plan Write for Pricing will help you choose a price to maximize profits or capture market share, evaluate sales potential and financial projections, clarify pricing objectives, and document your pricing strategy. For more information click the *Products* tab, then click Plan Write for Pricing on the Products page.

Professional Pricing Society

Website: http://www.pricingsociety.com

Keywords: Pricing Software and Tools

Description: Access the page described below to view providers of software and tools to help businesses price products and services. The information provided will give you a good idea of the products and services offered by each company listed.

Instructions: Click *Latest Pricing Software & Tools* in the center of the page toward the bottom.

17.18 PRODUCT EVALUATION

Quick Insight (QI)
(BRS Inc.)

Website: http://www.brs-inc.com/

Keywords: Product Evaluation Software

Description: Quick Insight is product evaluation software that will help you eval-uate critical business factors, produce a market assessment report, discover insights from an MBA level analysis and go to market with confidence. QI will help you evaluate the potential of a product before you make a major investment.

Click the *Products* tab at the top of the page to view a list of the products offered by BRS Inc.

17.19 PROJECT FUNDING

Sales Toolz Inc.

Website: http://www.salestoolz.com/

Keywords: Project Funding Information Product

Description: Sales Toolz Inc. offers a How to Get Your Project Funded E-learn-ing product. The product provides knowledge, understanding, practical examples and cost-benefit analysis software to help you get your product funded. It will also teach you the capital investment process that upper management uses to measure the potential returns on your proposed project.

For more information, click on *Products* then *E-learning*.

17.20 SALES PLANNING

Plan Write for Sales (BRS Inc.)

Website: http://www.brs-inc.com/

Keywords: Sales Planning Software

Description: Plan Write for Sales will help you analyze potential, develop a strategy around strengths and weaknesses, develop a comprehensive tactical plan, measure success and employ an action plan.

Click the *Products* tab at the top of the page to view a list of the products offered by BRS Inc.

17.21 SALES STRATEGY

Insight for Sales Strategy (BRS Inc.)

Website: http://www.brs-inc.com/

Keywords: Sales Strategy Software

Description: Insight for Sales Strategy will help you focus sales efforts, tailor sales to the needs of buyers, anticipate obstacles, enhance your current sales process and forecast sales accurately.

Click the *Products* tab at the top of the page to view a list of the products offered by BRS Inc.

17.22 SALES TOOLS

SiteSell.com

Website: http://www.sitesell.com/

Keywords: Tools to Sell Knowledge and Words
This company also offers products to help you sell from websites and auctions.

Description: SiteSell offers products to help websites and auction sites sell. This company also offers products to help you sell writing and knowledge.

To view SiteSell products, scroll to the bottom of the listed page and click on the item of interest.

17.23 SUPPLY CHAIN MANAGEMENT

Industrial Data & Information (IDII)

Website: http://www.idii.com/home.htm

Keywords: Supply Chain Software, Newsletter, Information and Resources

Description: If you're looking for information related to supply chain management software, this is good place to start. Its website contains a substantial amount of information about software used to manage supply chain operations.

17.24 SURVEY SOFTWARE

Survey Pro (Apian)

Website: http://www.apian.com/

Keywords: Survey Creation and Management Software

Description: SurveyPro offers a software solution for creating and managing surveys. The company's base package enables you to design paper questionnaires, enter or import data, and generate reports. You can purchase add-ons to help you with web, e-mail, LAN, kiosk, phone, and CD-related surveys. SurveyPro is a high-end product for medium-to-large-sized businesses or small businesses that do numerous surveys.

This company also offers Apian Survey Host services for web surveys.

The Survey System (Creative Research Systems)

Website: http://www.surveysystem.com/

Keywords: Survey Software, Basic to Advanced Options

Description: The Survey System by Creative Research Systems is available in basic, professional and enterprise editions. This company also offers optional modules to meet advanced needs. The products and options offered are designed to serve the needs of small-to-large businesses with respective needs and budgets.

Survey Software Forum

Website: http://pub40.ezboard.com/bsurveysoftwareforum

Keywords: Survey Software Forum

Description: The Survey Software Forum is a forum used by suppliers and end-users. Suppliers list their products, and users and researchers ask questions. If you have the time to post questions and check for replies, I'm sure you can get some valuable advice about survey software.

17.25 WEBSITE PROMOTION

Agent Web Ranking

Website: http://www.agentwebranking.com/

Keywords: Promotion Monitoring Software (search engine ranking)

Description: Agent Web Ranking monitors how your site is ranking on search engines. It automatically checks the visibility of websites on search engines and provides customized ranking reports. Agent Web Ranking is global software that works with and uses all of the major search engines and directories. Its search engine library is updated within 72 hours in the event that a search engine changes the way it displays results.

PromotionalSoftware.com

Website: http://www.promotionalsoftware.com/

Keywords: Website Promotion Software

Description: Promotionalsoftware.com features Web Position Gold 2 promotional software. You can download a trial version to try. Web Position Gold 2 is a leading software product for website promotion.

WordTracker

Website: http://www.wordtracker.com/

Keywords: Keyword Identification Software

Description: WordTracker identifies keywords to use when submitting a website to search engines. This service will help you identify the keyword combinations you should use. It will also help you understand the results you can expect with various search engines.

Using a service like the one offered by WordTracker will help you get higher rankings on search engines.

Search Engine Watch

Website: http://searchenginewatch.com/

Keywords: Search Engine Information and Resources

Description: Searchenginewatch.com features articles and information to help you understand how search engines work. This company provides submission tips to help you get your website noticed.

17.26 WEBSITE PROMOTION MANAGEMENT

E-centives

Website: http://www.ecentives.com/index.html

Keywords: Website Marketing Products

Description: E-centives offers an array of products and services to help you track customers, build databases, expand customer profiles, tailor offers, offer rewards, measure the success of promotions and more.

The services offered include strategic consulting and campaign management, user experience design and development services, analytics and data mining, and consumer acquisition.

17.27 SOFTWARE SELECTION SITES

Knowledgestorm.com

Website: http://www.knowledgestorm.com/

Keywords: Software Selection Site

Description: Looking for a specific type of software? Knowledgestorm.com enables you to search for 22,000-plus business-to-business software products and services. This company also provides information to help you research and compare solutions.

Software Marketing Resources

Website: http://www.softwaremarketingresource.com/

Keywords: Software Marketing Information

Description: The SMR website contains resources for software developers, publishers and user groups. Click on the graphic or the *Click Here* link to access the resource page.

Software Sites: The *Software Sites* link in the left column takes you to a page that lists numerous software-related websites. This page is an excellent place to look for freeware, shareware and software publisher websites.

Submission Tools: The *Submission Tools* link in the left column takes you to a page that lists numerous website submission and promotion applications.

Things to Remember

This section is a reminder of important types of resources. The resources in this section are listed throughout this guide. Additional listings under the following headings were added to illustrate their importance. Each of the headings in this section is followed by a short explanation to help you understand how the resources can be utilized.

Business and Marketing Advice
Business and Marketing-Related Services
Government & Organization Resources
Import/Export Resources
Industry Periodical Websites
Industry Specific Books & Information
Industry Specific Buyer's Guides
Industry Specific Websites
Trade Associations
Trade Shows

18.1 BUSINESS AND MARKETING ADVICE

If you need business or marketing advice, the following resources may be helpful. You can use them to find an answer to a question, or solution to a problem.

American List Counsel (ALC)

Website: http://www.amlist.com/

Keywords: Direct Mail and List Information

Description: The ALC Knowledge Center provides information related to data research, analysis, marketing and more. The company offers newsletters and reports, industry FAQs, a direct mail library, glossary of terms and an ask-an-expert service.

*Ask an Expert

Website: http://www.libraryspot.com/askanexpert.htm

Keywords: Questions or Problems? Ask an Expert Volunteer

Description: This website lists hundreds of professionals and volunteers willing to answer questions. If you need an answer to a question and don't know whom to ask, this website is a good place to start.

FIND SVP

Website: http://www.findsvp.com/default.cfm

Keywords: Knowledge Services Company

Description: Find SVP is a knowledge services company that offers a broad range of services of interest to marketers. Its one-time question answering option might be a service that saves the day. For $250, this firm will spend three hours finding an answer to a tough question. If you have a question or problem and can't find an answer anywhere else, this service may be worth trying.

*Service Corps of Retired Executives (SCORE)

Website: http://www.score.org/

Keywords: Business Advice and Counseling

Description: SCORE is a program sponsored by the U.S. Small Business Administration to assist small businesses. SCORE has 10,500 volunteer business counselors that provide small business mentoring and advice. You can get advice via e-mail or in person.

18.2 BUSINESS AND MARKETING-RELATED SERVICES

The following resources provide information and services to help you locate and manage service providers. You can use them to locate individuals and organizations that provide a variety of services. Some of them also offer services to help you manage and coordinate marketing projects.

BuyersZone.com

Website: http://www.buyerzone.com/index.html

Keywords: Marketing Services (purchasing information)

Description: Buyerszone.com offers information and services to help you purchase marketing services. When you click on a category, you're taken to a page that contains information and tips related to purchasing that type of service. The information to help you purchase marketing services is the most useful feature of this site.

This company also offers a service that enables you to get multiple quotes from multiple service providers. But, it does not offer comparable information about service providers.

*Elance

Website: http://www.elance.com/

Keywords: Marketing Services (purchasing)

Description: Visit the Elance website and select the *Elance Online* tab to view the services for small businesses. Elance connects buyers and service providers in hundreds of categories. Enter a job description and you'll receive bids from qualified service providers. You can also search for service providers by category and criteria selection.

Elance also offers *Elance Project Services*, which helps you with project scoping, vendor selection and/or project management assistance.

Kasamba

Website: http://www.kasamba.com/default.asp

Keywords: Locate Graphic Designers, Website Designers, Copywriters, etc.

Description: Kasamba is a good place to search for professionals to help you design graphics, logos, write sales copy, edit copy, etc. Its website enables you to search for professionals necessary to create brochures, logos, sales letters and more.

MarketIt Right

Website: http://www.marketitright.com/

Keywords: Marketing Project Coordination and Resources

Description: MarketIt Right is an intermediary service for businesses and marketing-related service providers. This service works to automate marketing communications planning and implementation for businesses.

The services this company provides and coordinates are extensive. It streamlines the planning process and brings marketers and service providers together.

Portfolio.com

Website: http://www.portfolios.com/

Keywords: Locate Design and Copy Professionals

Description: Portfolio.com is a great place to find a design or copy professional. You can search for graphic designers, copywriters, photographers, industrial designers, illustrators, animators and more.

This service is free to users. The registered service providers pay for listings.

Writing Assistance Inc.

Website: http://www.writingassist.com/index.htm

Keywords: Contract and Permanent Communications Professionals

Description: Writing Assistance Inc. is an employment agency for communications professionals. This firm will help you find technical writers, marketing communications writers, training developers, project managers, website designers, content developers and graphic designers.

18.3 GOVERNMENT & ORGANIZATION RESOURCES

If you're on a limited budget and need assistance to develop a marketing or business plan, don't forget the government and organizational resources that are available. The U.S. Government and other organizations offer a variety of programs and services for small business owners. For information about other government resources, see the *Government Information section.*

*International Trade Centre

Website: http://www.intracen.org/

Keywords: International Trade and Business Information

Description: The World Trade Organization (WTO) and the United Nations (UN) operate the International Trade Centre. The ITC website contains information related to product and market development, development of trade support services, trade information, human resource development, international purchasing and supply management, needs assessment, and program design for trade promotion.

The ITC offers an abundant amount of quality information and resources for anyone wanting to do business internationally.

*Service Corps of Retired Executives (SCORE)

Website: http://www.score.org/

Keywords: Business Advice and Counseling

Description: SCORE is a program sponsored by the U.S. Small Business Administration to assist small businesses. Score has 10,500 volunteer business counselors that provide small business mentoring and advice. You can get advice via e-mail or in person.

Small Business Administration (SBA)

Website: http://www.sba.gov/library/pubs.html

Keywords: Business Information and Services

Description: The SBA offers a variety of business and marketing information. Its publications page lists a variety of information related to business and marketing.

If you're a small business owner on a limited budget, don't forget to check out the various services that the SBA offers.

Small Business Development Centers

Website: http://www.asbdc-us.org/

Keywords: Business Development Advice and Resources

Description: The Association of Small Business Development Centers' website enables you to locate small business development centers. The *Lead Centers* link at the top of the page takes you to a page where you can search for SBDCs by state.

If you're starting a new business or need information about running a business, check to see if there is a SBDC in your area.

U.S. Business Advisor

Website: http://www.business.gov/busadv/index.cfm

Keywords: Business Assistance, International Trade

Description: The U.S. Business Advisor website contains information and resources related to business development, financial assistance, laws and regulations, international trade, buying and selling, agencies and gateways, e-services, learning the Internet and more.

Click on the *Agencies and Gateways* link to view a scrolling list of government agencies and information sources.

The e-services link takes you to a page of articles, links and information related to doing business online.

18.4 IMPORT/EXPORT RESOURCES

The *International Business section* contains numerous import/export resources. The following are a good place to start if you're interested in importing/exporting products or services.

Import Administration

Website: http://ia.ita.doc.gov/

Keywords: Import Information and Related Data

Description: The Import Administration website contains information and data for importers, exporters, individuals, and organizations interested in doing business internationally. It provides links to government data on importing, adminis-trative protective orders, antidumping, currency exchange rates, a document library, expected wages, federal register notices, glossary of terms and phrases, laws and regulations, statistics, USDOC person finder and more.

Export.gov

Website: http://www.export.gov/index.html

Keywords: Export Information and Services (excellent site)

Description: The Small Business Administration operates Export.gov. Its website contains information and resources of interest to individuals and organizations interested in selling products or services in other countries. You can find informa-tion related to export counseling, export promotion programs and services, coun-try and industry market research, finance and insurance trade agreements, trade statistics, trade events, export basics, foreign currency rates, international con-tacts, industry sector offices and contacts, tariffs and taxes, export documenta-tion, U.S. export controls, schedule B (shipper's export declaration), NAFTA rules of origin, foreign trade advocacy, export assistance offices worldwide, etc.

Subscription Services: You can subscribe to the Export.gov newsletter and sign up for webcasts on exporting. You can also access the organization's archive of Export.gov newsletters.

18.5 INDUSTRY-SPECIFIC BOOKS & INFORMATION

Throughout my research, I've found numerous books related to marketing spe-cific types of products or services. People that operated successful businesses wrote many of them.

Booksellers such as iUniverse.com or Amazon.com are excellent places to search for industry-specific titles. If you need ideas, try searching for a title related to marketing the type of product or service you offer. You might be surprised at what you'll find.

The following are also good resources to find specific types of information and books.

Bowker's Global Books in Print

Website: http://www.globalbooksinprint.com/

Keywords: Book Search Site (global)

Description: The Bowker's Books in Print website is a good place to do an extensive search for available publications. It is a great place to find publications related to a foreign country or specific subject.

You'll have to sign up for a courtesy trial to use the site's features.

*Means Business

Website: http://www.meansbusiness.com/default.asp

Keywords: Business Information (aggregated information from published books)

Description: MeansBusiness aggregates information that is hand picked by business editors. This service helps users find the best information from the best books related to a specific subject.

Click a topic in the right column to access a page that lists summaries and related sub-topics. If you see a title or subject that interests you, click on it. You'll be taken to page where you can view short summaries or choose to buy a full summary.

This is a great service. It enables you to find the information you need without having to read numerous books.

National Technical Information Service (NTIS)

Website: http://www.ntis.gov/

Keywords: Government Information Search Site
(search for over 750,000 publications)

Description: Publications like the *U.S. Industry & Trade Outlook* and the *Statistical Abstract of the United States* can be found and ordered at the listed website. Many publications can be downloaded directly from the site. I used the search mechanism for a while and wasn't real impressed. It is, however, sufficient to find common government publications.

Sample Search Results: I entered *marketing* and *computers* in the NTIS advanced search feature and 7702 results were found. After the first page, the listed results were very relevant. The second page listed reports on computer-related exports to numerous countries.

18.6 INDUSTRY-SPECIFIC BUYERS GUIDES

The following resource lists industry-specific buyers guides. If you buy or sell a specific type of product, a related buyers guide might be a valuable resource.

Software Marketing Resources

Website: http://www.softwaremarketingresource.com/

Keywords: Links to Industry-Specific Buyers Guides

Description: Click on the *Click Here* link toward the bottom left corner to enter the site. The *Buyers Guides* link in the left navigation bar takes you to a page that has links for industry-specific buyers guides. This site is a good place to start if you're looking for industry-specific products and services.

18.7 INDUSTRY-SPECIFIC WEBSITES

Industry specific websites often contain valuable links, resources and information. If you want to locate an industry-specific website, Online-pr.com is a good place to start.

Online-pr.com

Website: http://www.online-pr.com/

Keywords: Industry-Specific Websites

Description: The websites you can access from this page are good. It is a good starting point to locate websites that offer industry-specific information.

18.8 MAGAZINE & PERIODICAL WEBSITES

The websites operated by magazine and periodical publishers are generally good information sources. They feature a variety information and resources related to specific interests. The following resources will help you locate periodicals related to specific products, services and industries.

American Journalism Review (AJR)

Website: http://www.ajr.org/

Keywords: Periodical Searches/Media Searches

Description: If you need to find an industry-specific periodical or general media source, this site is a good place to start. It lists newspapers, magazines, television networks, radio stations and more.

FindArticles.com

Website: http://www.findarticles.com/cf_0/PI/index.jhtml

Keywords: Article Search Tool

Description: FindArticles.com is an excellent place to find specific types of articles. I searched for multicultural marketing information and found an array of articles from leading sources.

FindArticles.com contains articles from more than 300 magazines and journals. You'll find articles related to business, health, society, entertainment, sports and more. You can read entire articles and print them at no cost.

Gebbie Press

Website: http://www.gebbieinc.com/

Keywords: Media Search Website

Description: The Gebbie Press website enables you to search for the websites of newspapers, TV stations, radio stations and magazines. The magazine search tool enables you to search for periodicals by subject. Select a subject to see a list of related periodicals. Click on a specific periodical to view its website.

Magazine and periodical websites are generally good sources of information. After finding these sites, you may want to bookmark them or save them as favorites for easy access.

To find a media-related website, select the media type under Media Links at the bottom of the left navigation bar.

*Media Finder

Website: http://www.mediafinder.com/

Keywords: Media Locator (newspapers, magazines, newsletters, etc.)

Description: Media Finder is an excellent media locator service. To view the full listings, you'll have to subscribe to the service. If you don't subscribe, you'll have to locate the websites and contact information yourself.

Your local library is another option. Most libraries carry a print version of The Standard Periodical Directory, which is published by Oxbridge Communications, Inc.

News Directory

Website: http://www.newsdirectory.com/

Keywords: Find Newspapers, Magazines and TV Stations

Description: The News Directory website enables you search for media sources. You can perform searches by title or area code. You can also search by selecting a subject or country.

NewsLink

Website: http://newslink.org/

Keywords: National and International Media Companies

Description: Newslink.org is a good place to find industry-specific periodicals or general media sources. Its website enables you to search for media-related sources throughout the world. It lists magazines, newspapers, and radio/TV stations.

A limited number of magazines were listed in some of the categories I searched.

18.9 TRADE ASSOCIATIONS

If you're marketing a product or service in an established industry, check for related trade associations. Trade associations offer valuable information related to specific products, services, industries and interests. Many of them offer industry-specific periodicals and publications.

ASAE (American Society of Association Executives)

Website: http://info.asaenet.org/gateway/OnlineAssocSlist.html

Keywords: Association Search Site

Description: If you need to find a specific type of trade association, the ASAE website is a good place to start. Simply type in a subject or keyword in the *Associ-*

ation Name Contains search box and press go. This site also gives you the option of specifying categories and region. It contains thousands of listings and is very functional.

*Federation of International Trade Associations (FITA)

Website: http://www.fita.org/index.html

Keywords: Trade Associations, Market Research Resources, etc.

Description: FITA has a great website. It has an index of 4,000 web resources, international market research resources, articles about international trade, a directory of international trade associations in North America, directory of export management companies and more.

The fita.org website is well-organized and easy to use. It contains a vast amount of useful information for anyone doing business globally.

The Trade Association Forum (U.K.)

Website: http://www.taforum.org/searchgroup.pl?n=500

Keywords: U.K. Trade Association Search Site

Description: If you need to find a U.K. trade association, this website is a good place to start. Follow the instructions at the top of the page to locate U.K. trade associations.

18.10 TRADE SHOWS

Attending industry trade shows is a good way to promote products and services. They're also a great place to meet related professionals.

You can use the TSEA website to locate various types of trade shows, information and related resources.

*Trade Show News Network (TSNN)

Website: http://www2.tsnn.com/

Keywords: Trade Show-Related Information and Resources

Description: The TSNN website enables you to search for trade shows and related suppliers. You can also list and search for products and services in various categories. The site gives you access to resources, publications, related associations, international trade show information and more.

There is a vast amount of information, resources and services featured on this site.

*TradeShow Week

Website: http://www.tradeshowweek.com/

Keywords: Trade Show Information, Searches and Related Articles

Description: The TradeShow Week website enables you to search for industry-specific trade shows and related information. Click the *Tradeshow Directory* link to search for industry trade shows around the world.

The *Article Archives* link takes you to a page where you can search for related articles. You can also search for related products and services by clicking the *Buyers Guide* link.

Publications: Tradeshow Week and related directories

Glossary Resources

19.1 INTERNATIONAL ECONOMICS

Deardorff's Glossary of International Economics

Website: http://www-personal.umich.edu/~alandear/glossary/

Keywords: International Economics Terminology and Definitions

Description: The listed website provides definitions for words and terms related to international economics.

19.2 MAIL ORDER TERMINOLOGY

Mail Order Dictionary

Website: http://www.howtoadvice.com/MailOrderDictionary

Keywords: Mail Order Terminology

Description: Wondering what a mail order-related term or phrase means? The mail order dictionary defines basic words and terms commonly associated with mail order.

19.3 MARKETING TERMINOLOGY

Dictionary of Marketing Terms

Website: http://www.marketingpower.com

Keywords: Dictionary of Marketing Terms

Description: The Dictionary of Marketing Terms is an AMA Publication (American Marketing Association). It's an excellent reference guide that will help you understand marketing terminology. It contains a lot of useful information.

To find the periodicals and publications available from the AMA website, select the *Site Map* link at the top or bottom of the page. Some pages do not have a *Site Map* link at the bottom of the page.

Once you've opened the site map page, click on *Publications* under the AMA Info sub-heading. It takes you to a page that lists and describes pages with periodicals, journals, and books.

Landor

Website: http://www.landor.com/

Keywords: Branding Dictionary and Articles

Description: Click on the *What is Branding?* link at the top of the page. From the *What is Branding?* page, you can access the Branding Dictionary and Branding Articles. The articles on this site are good. The branding dictionary provides short definitions of common terms related to branding.

19.4 WEB & INTERNET TERMINOLOGY

Netlingo

Website: http://www.netlingo.com/searchstation.cfm

Keywords: Internet, Web, and Chat Room Terminology

Description: If you don't know what a word or term related to the Internet or web means, this website can help. You can search by category or keyword. You can also browse for definitions alphabetically.

19.5 WEB MARKETING TERMINOLOGY

E-commerce & Marketing Dictionary

Website: http://www.udel.edu/alex/dictionary.html

Keywords: E-commerce and Marketing Dictionary

Description: Need to find out what a web or Internet-related term or abbreviation means? This website is an easy to use quick loading site that lets you search for definitions in alphabetical order. If you can't find what you need at this site, scroll to the bottom of the page and try one of the other resources listed.

Interactive Advertising Bureau (IAB)

Website: http://www.iab.net/resources/glossary.asp

Keywords: Glossary of Interactive Advertising Terms

Description: The IAB website lets you search for definitions to terms and abbreviations related to web and interactive advertising.

If you have problems accessing this page, go to http://www.iab.net/ and type *glossary* in the search box and click go. Then click on one of the entries listed.

MarketingTerms.com

Website: http://www.marketingterms.com/

Keywords: Internet and Web-Related Marketing Terms and Definitions

Description: Marketingterms.com defines hundreds of terms and words related to web marketing. This is a great site. It's well organized and easy to use.

Conclusion

I hope that the Marketing Yellow Pages have helped you find the resources you need to succeed.

My goal was to make this publication useful and affordable. I wanted to create a publication that would help individuals and small businesses find the resources they needed to successfully market products and services. I also wanted it to be affordable.

The second edition of this guide will have features to make it more useful. The table of contents will be expanded to help different types of businesses find the resources they need. Features will also be added to help differentiate various products and services.

Additional resources and expanded resource descriptions will also be added to the second edition. The number of resources in most categories will be increased and additional categories will be added to help you find resources that are specific to your needs.

The success of small businesses and individuals is what the Marketing Yellow Pages are about. My goal is to make each new edition an improved resource to help small businesses succeed.

If you have questions, comments or concerns please feel free to write.

Send Questions or Comments to:

MYP
PO Box 2694
Casper, WY 82602

0-595-28132-X

www.ingramcontent.com/pod-product-compliance
Lightning Source LLC
Chambersburg PA
CBHW020740180526
45163CB00001B/290